THE HISTORY OF
DEATH

BURIAL CUSTOMS AND FUNERAL RITES, FROM THE ANCIENT WORLD TO MODERN TIMES

Michael Kerrigan

The Lyons Press

Guilford, Connecticut
An imprint of The Globe Pequot Press

10 9 8 7 6 5 4 3 2 1

Printed in Dubai, UAE

Editorial and design by:
Amber Books Ltd
Bradley's Close
74-77 White Lion Street
London N1 9PF
United Kingdom
www.amberbooks.co.uk

Project Editor: Sarah Uttridge
Design: Graham Curd
Picture Research: Kate Green and Terry Forshaw

ISBN: 978-1-59921-201-2

Library of Congress Cataloging-in-Publication Data is available on file.

Contents

INTRODUCTION

The attempt to gain knowledge of the past is also a journey into the world of the dead,' writes the Italian cultural scholar Carlo Ginzburg. If this is indeed the case, then this book is embarking on a doubly adventurous voyage, setting out as it does to explore the history of death itself. Something that proverbially comes to us all, death is universal and yet universally strange, an object of fascination and of fear. Elaborate rituals have become associated with death, life's culmination or the moment of its extinction – as if we hope, by stage-managing it, to moderate its force.

Ancient cultures freely personified death, a power they struggled to understand – hence the various deities, vengeful or welcoming, of early times. More recent societies created allegorical figures, like the Grim Reaper with his swinging scythe, to embody the awesome cruelty of death. Advances in modern science have given us unprecedented abilities to direct our physical destiny, but in the face of death we seem as helpless as we ever were. One by one, death's various physiological processes have been fathomed, but for many people the meaning of death seems to remain out of reach.

THE HOUR OF OUR DEATH?

One of the eternal verities of life, death unites us all across the ages: there are many ancient civilizations we know about only through their tombs. Yet, for

Left: The people of Ambalamana, Madagascar process round their village in the ceremony of *famadihana*, the 'turning of the bones', 1994.

Inset: For centuries chillingly familiar as a symbol of mortality, the 'Grim Reaper' cuts his harvest of human life.

7

Right: Prayer stones mark
an area set aside for
Buddhist 'sky burials' in
Lhu Chu canyon, high up
in the mountains of Tibet.

something that is a constant of human existence, there has been surprisingly little agreement on what death is, or what it represents. That so many different societies, in so many centuries, should have had their own ways and rituals of death is not perhaps surprising – after all, they have had their own ways and rituals of life. But there has not even been a full consensus on the precise moment at which death can be said to happen, the instant at which – as some cultures (though by no means all) would have it – the body becomes a mere carcass and the soul takes flight. Jewish scholars have been debating since Talmudic times whether the indication of death should be taken from the breath or from the pulse, for example, and there is no sign of the dispute being satisfactorily resolved. Strict Hindus hold that death does not actually take place until the skull splits in the extreme heat of the funeral pyre.

In many cultures, however, the deceased was not considered to be truly dead until the decomposition of the body was completed. Thus a practice still prevails on several of the outlying islands of Indonesia of holding second funerals at which the skeletal remains – now bare of flesh – can be properly reburied. A similar view underlies the Madagascan tradition of *famadihana,* the ritual exhumation of the dead, and the 'turning of their bones' for final burial. (The disinterred bones may be paraded around the village and 'shown' the changes that have taken place since the person died. Hence they will be up-to-date with all the news when they are laid in the earth for the last time.) The same perspective may well have been implicit in the tradition of North America's Lakota Sioux, who placed the bodies of their deceased on platforms in trees, to be picked clean by birds and animals prior to their final interment in the ground in skeletal form. Several Australian Aboriginal tribes exposed their dead in much the same way.

Zoroastrian tradition holds that the soul does not leave the body and ascend to heaven at the moment of death, but rather hovers in its vicinity for three days before beginning its journey to the afterlife. This period in limbo would have roughly coincided with the time taken by crows and vultures to eat the flesh from a body left out on one of the specially built 'Towers of Silence', which are still to be seen around Iran. 'Sky burials' continue to take place in Tibet: bodies are left out on rocky outcrops to be reduced to skeletons by scavenging birds.

All these customs suggest a belief in some intermediate state between life and death, an idea that finds explicit formulation in the ancient Tibetan idea of bardo. The event that Western cultures call 'death' is, according to the *Bardo Thodol,* or Tibetan Book of the Dead, only the beginning of a transition – the first stage, or *chikhai bardo.* The body may be inert, but the person is only in a state of trance, and can still be reached by the prayers of the living. Four days will pass before the person progresses to the second stage, or *chonyid bardo,* at which point the departed is confronted by a radiant light. The purest will rush to greet it, the flawed will have to flee. It is only now that the realization dawns on the dead person that death has occurred, and the events of their recent life on earth are reviewed in a series of visions. The dead person now progresses towards the third stage, the *sidpa bardo,* in the course of which death merges imperceptibly with birth, as the body moves towards its incarnation in another body for another life.

In many cultures the deceased was not considered to be truly dead until the decomposition of the body was completed.

Above: In Celebes (Sulawesi, Indonesia), graves cut into the bare rock house little dolls representing the deceased of the Toraja people.

IN THE FAMILY

In Toraja, Sulawesi, one of the islands of Indonesia, the dead are not buried at all, but sit for months in temporary houses while they slowly rot. In some cases, they may even be given a seat in some corner of the family home, well wrapped with fabric to soak up the juices of decay. Within a few days, the worst of the smell has gone and the departed relative becomes a part of the domestic furniture, a welcome presence in the bosom of the family by whom they were loved. Grotesque though this may seem from a modern, Western point of view, the reasoning behind this practice would have been well understood by many other cultures. Indeed, scholars speculate that the famous Fayyum portraits may have been made for a similar purpose. Found in Fayyum, south of Cairo, these painted faces were created by the Romano-Egyptian society of the first and second centuries AD. Lovingly painted, and strikingly modern in the warmth and softness with which they are delineated, they may have been used to lend a human presence to bodies mummified in the traditional Egyptian way. The theory goes that these too would have been displayed within the home for several months before they were buried, so that the dead would have a continuing presence among the living.

Once Toraja's dead have decayed sufficiently, their bones are laid to rest in tombs – as prestigious as the family can manage. Life-sized carved wooden figures, known as *tau tau,* are set on guard outside. These serve both as sentinels and as reminders of the departed dead: for centuries they were strongly stylized in form, but are now far more naturalistic, as befits an age of photography and TV. The enduring existence of such figures can be seen as just another way in which the boundary between life and death is more elusive in many cultures than it has come to seem in the societies of the modern developed world.

For students of death rituals, there is indeed no more fruitful source than Indonesia, an archipelago in whose scattered islands many different cultures have evolved separately over centuries. An enormous cultural diversity has developed over a comparatively small geographical area, and the islands contain a collection of customs quite different from those to be found anywhere else in the world. Funerary traditions often seem particularly exotic to outsiders. They are typically extravagant – not just figuratively, in unbridled ceremonial and colour, but literally, in terms of sheer expense. The spectacle is such that in

Sumba it has come to be accepted that an important funeral is too big an occasion to be missed – even by the individual whose funeral it is. Hence there is the situation in which a wealthy islander is likely to attend his own obsequies, which are held while he is alive. From a Western perspective, this may appear preposterous, but where the border between life and death is less clear cut, such an attitude seems logical enough.

Many cultures make death-masks, which may be displayed to perpetuate the image of the departed among the living; this also helps blur the boundary between the two states. Marriages between living men and women and ghosts figure almost routinely in Native American mythology – most often, a man or woman discovers that he or she has for years been married to a phantom. A different sort of 'ghost marriage', however, may take place in some Sudanese societies. When important men have died without issue, threatening their lineage with extinction, living stand-ins may father children in their name. Among the Singapore Chinese, the tradition that young men and women should not marry before their elder brothers or sisters have been wed causes obvious problems when those older siblings have died before their time. In these circumstances, the dead brothers and sisters are often married off to one another, clearing the way for further marriages to take place among the living. Among the Karo Batak of Sumatra, it is reported, young boys and girls whose lives are cut short before they

Left: Death-masks gave the spirit of the deceased an enduring physical form. This mask is a Mayan one, from southeastern Mexico.

have passed through life's appointed stages are ritually 'married' so that they may fulfil their proper destiny. The boy's penis may be enclosed in a piece of bamboo and the girl penetrated with a banana to indicate the consummation of this marriage.

DEATH AND REBIRTH

If all these different traditions seem strange and exotic, it is important to appreciate how far modern medicine has rendered the idea of death ambiguous for every one of us. The notion of 'brain death' is a very recent one, and patients may now be kept on artificial 'life support' long after their 'life' (as we would normally understand the word) is over. The moral and psychological implications of such developments are far-reaching: never before have we had even the illusion of being able to control the passage of the living person into the realm of death. Mutterings about doctors 'playing God' make clear how uneasy we are about these changes. In fact, the more awesome responsibility may end up devolving not on the medical professionals but onto relatives. They might be asked to decide whether what may seem a very diminished version of a life should be sustained, or whether the life-support machine should be shut down and that existence snuffed out.

It is important to appreciate how far modern medicine has rendered the idea of death ambiguous for every one of us.

Yet many cultures – perhaps most – do not see death as something final, and some regard it as no more than the transition to other earthly lives. The idea of reincarnation has played a part in several religious traditions, but is especially associated with certain Indian creeds like Hinduism, Buddhism and Jainism. Briefly, these see life as a continuing, swirling cycle of death and rebirth, known traditionally by the Sanskrit word *samsara* (literally, 'wandering'). The *atnam* or *jiva,* as the soul is known, 'transmigrates' from one living form to another, animal or human, at a lower or higher level of existence according to how well or badly each life has been lived. The principle of *karma,* which translates as 'action' or 'deed', governs the relative placing of these successive lives: what we do in this life will have a bearing on where we lead the next. In the words of the Brhadaranaka Upanishad: 'Whoso does good actions becomes good; whoso does evil actions becomes evil. Whatever karma he does, that he attains.' The soul that has lived badly will take the 'southern path' or the 'way of the fathers' when this life ends and lead its next life a level or so lower. The good soul follows the 'way of the gods', and leads its next life at a higher level. Buddhism recognizes six of these *gati,* or levels of existence, ranging from gods through demigods, mortal humans and animals to ghosts and the damned in hell. The ultimate goal of living is to escape altogether this endless chain of action and consequence. For Hindus, this means shrugging off earthly feelings and concerns to arrive at that utter purity of essence known as *brahman* – a quality clearly akin to that of the highest Buddhist enlightenment, nirvana. Both see the blissful soul as existing in an exalted state, beyond the reach of time, mortality or the preoccupations of the world.

The Greek philosopher and mathematician Pythagoras, who lived during the sixth century BC, was famously a believer in the transmigration of souls. Such a belief may have been widespread in his society – in the mythology of the Greeks, the twins Castor and Pollux were both metamorphosed into stars. And this despite an 'official' Greek tradition, evidenced elsewhere in Classical myths, that

Right: In his erotic verse, 'death' implies orgasm; in his religious verse ('Death be not proud…') an end for the faithful to prepare for but not to fear. John Donne exemplifies the ambivalence of the Jacobean attitude to death.

the dead were rowed across one or other of the subterranean rivers, the Styx or the Acheron, by the boatman Charon to their final destination in the kingdom of Hades. Neither account fits in with the Greek stories of the Hesperides or Isles of the Blessed (associated with the Canaries) or, for that matter, with other accounts in which heroes spend eternity in the ease and tranquillity of the Elysian Fields. Many cultures contain elements of 'syncretism', the grafting together of diverse traditions, so such apparent contradictions should come as no surprise.

FUNERARY FUN

We are, perhaps, all confused in certain aspects of our response to death. Different societies disagree strongly over whether it is a sad and solemn event, or one to be met with quiet satisfaction that the departed has gone on to 'a better place', or even celebrated with uproarious revelry. For the Betsileo of Madagascar, the funeral is the occasion of a riotous carnival of drunkenness and general licence. Anarchic battles between men and bulls are held, but such disorders are nothing to the moral abandonment that is allowed once the 'mourners' have covered their faces with the shrouds of the dead, symbolically blinding themselves and veiling their behaviour from the gods. In that state, they are unaccountable to any of the normal constraints and taboos, and even incestuous sex between brothers and sisters is allowed.

The association between sex and death has long been taken for granted, though not understood. Elizabethan English poets such as John Donne used the word 'die' as a synonym for orgasm. Sigmund Freud famously theorized what the popular imagination already took for granted, albeit unconsciously, when he yoked together the principles of *eros,* or sexual love, and *thanatos,* the 'death instinct'. Beleaguered as we are by the tensions and frustrations of life, we yearn at some level for escape into extinction – Freud himself likened this to the Buddhist concept of nirvana. The moment of sexual release (in French, traditionally, *petite mort,* or 'little death') offers us an intimation, however transitory, of this blissful state. In old Russia, and in other Slavic countries, the same sort of celebrations were held for funerals as for weddings, underlining this imaginative association.

Sometimes, though, the funerary festivities seem to have been intended more simply, to banish the fear of death. In many old Slavic communities, mock funerals (sometimes with real bodies) were a centrepiece of the Christmas frivolities. In pagan times, of course, the winter festival was held to mark the symbolic 'death' of the sun at the solstice. As an entertainment, it helped to keep at bay the darkness of the season's shortest days, and as a ritual, its purpose was to summon back the sun, restoring fertility to the earth that had apparently been abandoned. To hold a burlesque funeral, then, making fun of the idea of death, must have provided reassurance in a time of deep unease.

Western European cultures may not have taken funereal fun to such extremes, but this does not necessarily mean that obsequies were always staid affairs. The wake was in its origins a prayerful vigil by the coffin of the dead, on the night before its burial, but the Irish wake became by tradition a raucous party. Stereotypically, the English approach to death has been more sober, but a hint of comic irreverence survives in the tradition of the comic epitaph – that of the eighteenth-century highwayman, Claude Duvall, for instance. He was hanged in

Elizabethan English poets like John Donne used the word 'die' as a synonym for orgasm.

1670, despite the protests of the ladies of the court, with whom the dashing young gentleman-robber had been a favourite. He was buried in St Paul's, Covent Garden, London, and his gravestone (sadly lost in a fire of 1795), read:

> Here lies Du Vall: Reader, if male thou art,
> Look to thy purse: if female to thy heart.

A wry, 'black' humour became the norm for epitaphs of this kind, such as that inscribed in St Augustine's church, West Monkton, Somerset, for village doctor William Kinglake:

> Contention's doubtful
> Where two champions bee;
> Thou hast conquered Death;
> Now Death hath conquered thee.

The comic epitaph, indeed, became a sort of literary genre that reached its height in the 1700s – verses were written for sheer amusement as much as for actual use. When the poet John Gay died in 1732, for example, he was given the Westminster Abbey burial that was seen as befitting his distinction. His own, self-scripted, epitaph, would never have done:

> Life is a jest and all things show it,
> I thought so once but now I know it.

When two young sweethearts, John Hewet and Sarah Drew, were killed by lightning while helping with the harvest in the Oxfordshire village of Stanton Harcourt in 1718, the poet Alexander Pope was staying nearby. He was moved to pen a fittingly solemn verse to the couple's memory but also a less decorous couplet for the amusement of his friends:

> Here lye two poor Lovers who had the mishap,
> Tho very chaste People, to die of a Clap.

Punning, of course, on the two senses of 'clap', as a clap of thunder and as a dose of gonorrhoea, this rhyme is at once enjoyably witty and cruelly distasteful. In an extreme way, then, it exemplifies an ambivalence to be found running through the entire genre.

The staid Victorians frowned upon such levity, and the comic epitaph became a 'lost tradition', to be rediscovered by the humorists of the twentieth century. Today, quirky epitaphs abound in dictionaries of quotations and popular websites; that the majority will never actually have been inscribed on gravestones is beside the point. The same was often true, as we have seen, in the epitaph's heyday during the eighteenth century. Of more interest is the enduring appeal of these playful verses and the light-hearted view they take of what is officially such a serious subject. Epitaphs are enjoyable from a literary perspective because they offer us everything from elegant irony to withering social satire – all distilled into just a couple of lines or so. Perhaps their most important function, however, is to make fun of the thing we most fear, giving us some sense of poise and control in our approach to the idea of death.

BEYOND UNDERSTANDING

Death, says Shakespeare's Hamlet, is 'the undiscovered country': in the end, we feel, we do not understand our final destiny. Men and women have been struggling to comprehend death throughout recorded history – and no doubt they were struggling to comprehend it long before, or at least to rationalize it. Over 4000 years ago, in the Sumerian states of Mesopotamia, the story of Adapa was told. His name literally means 'man', so this figure is what we might call 'Everyman', the archetype for every human who came after. The Adapa of the myth, however, was a priest and a fisherman, whose boat was sunk in a storm one day. In his frustration, he attacked the south wind with curses. Some days later, An, the god of the heavens, realized that the wind had stopped blowing and asked his minions why: they told him that Adapa's verbal assault had broken the wind's wing. An sent for Adapa who, awed at the prospect of meeting the great god, asked Ea, the god of water, for his counsel.

Ea recommended that he dress himself in mourning before presenting himself before Dumuzi and Gizzida, the guardian-gods at the gates of heaven. When asked the reason for this garb, he should explain that he was grief-stricken at the

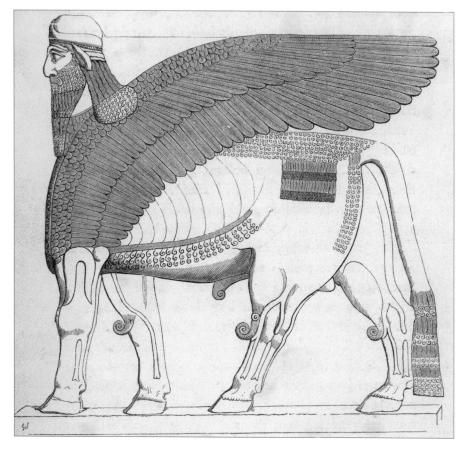

Left: With the body of a bull, a raptor's wings and a stern and unforgiving human head, this Mesopotamian god was unlikely to show much pity for mere mortals.

Every culture has died a little differently, just as it has found different ways of living life.

deaths of Dumuzi and Gizzida themselves. They would be so tickled by this absurdity that they would speed Adapa through into the presence of the great god An, and even put in a good word for him. An, Ea continued, would most likely offer him gifts of oil and a robe – which he should accept. But he should politely refuse any offer of bread and water.

So it turned out: Dumuzi and Gizzida were duly delighted at the joke, and in no time at all Adapa was standing before An's throne. As predicted, the great deity offered him a meal of bread and water, along with a robe and oil which he recommended that he throw away. Instead, to An's astonishment, Adapa insisted on shrouding and anointing himself for death – and rejecting the bread and water of eternal life. Sadly, he shook his head, as he saw the representative of humankind – the willing dupe of the evil Ea – deliberately spurning the greatest gift any god could give.

The Caddo, a native people from what is now eastern Texas in the United States, give a very different account of the origin of death. To begin with, their traditional story goes, there was no such thing as death. However, babies kept being born, and the earth was soon impossibly full with people. The tribal elders met to discuss the situation, and the suggestion was put forward that it might be a good idea if people should die for a time, and return to earth a little later. The Coyote came to the meeting, and he was impatient with such half-measures: if people died only temporarily, he argued, this would merely store up troubles for later. The population would continue growing in their absence and, as soon as they returned, the world would face the worst of crises, for there would not be the food for so many hungry mouths. In the face of this argument, the Council could not agree; whilst there might be much in what Coyote said, they could not willingly accept that their loved ones should be lost irrevocably. It was decided, therefore, that the dead should be gone for just a while, before returning to join the living.

A large 'medicine house' was accordingly built as the place to which the departed spirits would be summoned by the song of the priest once their sojourn in the realm of death was at an end. When the first man died, the priests waited 10 days before gathering to call his spirit back. He was seen, a whirlwind blowing in from far off across the western sky. As he neared the house, however, Coyote suddenly shut the door. Thwarted, the tornado went on its way to oblivion. From that time on, death has been a permanent state; the Caddo have seen tornadoes as the wandering souls of the dead – and the Coyote has been shunned, an outcast from all decent society.

THE FINISHING LINE

Death may be universal, but that does not mean that it is always and everywhere the same. On the contrary, it has taken on aspects of the extraordinary variety of human existence. Every culture has died a little differently, just as it has found different ways of living life. There are some clear constants, though. Most civilizations have feared death, despite the various forms of salvation on offer from their priests. Ultimately – again, despite the claims of religion to explain its workings – most peoples have found death difficult to comprehend. The pain of bereavement has always been acute, however much it may have been tempered by the faith that the departed has gone to lead a better life elsewhere. Faith may well do much to hearten the dying and those who mourn their passing, but it is a formidable faith indeed that never falters.

And yet, we remain fatalistic – if for no other reason than a lack of choice. For death, we know, will come to us all one day. Medical advances and modern welfare provision have done much to boost life expectancies in developed societies, whose citizens now live well over twice as long on average as those of Athens in its golden age. And while few in Old Testament times can really have managed the vaunted biblical lifespan of 'three score years and ten', modern health care has made it a realistic aspiration. Yet by prolonging life, we understand, we do not abolish death but merely postpone the inevitable.

So, stoicism makes a certain sense – and is not without its comforts. The chief of these, perhaps, is the feeling of 'closure' that death brings. 'From hence the lesson draw', wrote Sophocles in the concluding lines of his classic tragedy *Oedipus Tyrannus* in the fifth century BC:

> To reckon no man happy till ye see
> The closing day; until he pass the bourn
> Which severs life from death, unscathed
> by woe.

The implication is clear: only in its end does life find definition, and only in its conclusion does the narrative attain its final shape. If any single assumption has underpinned the bewildering array of rituals and beliefs that have accrued around death down the ages, it is perhaps this sense of death as the closure that completes the life. Hence the importance attached to this final ritual, the need for everything to be just right. A modern rationalist may wish to argue that a corpse is just decaying matter, but few in human history have shared this view. How much the dead themselves benefit from all the sacrifices, sacraments, processions, prayers, tombs and the other paraphernalia of death is, of course, debatable. It might be claimed that such things are 'really' done for the sake of the survivors. In the end, of course, it hardly matters: we live the lives our culture has prepared us for, and die the deaths our lives have led us to. But it appears to be an eternal principle that, whatever society – and whatever century – we may live in, our sense of decorum in death is one of the things that makes life worth living.

Below: The tragedies of Sophocles (495–406 BC) bear moving testimony to the stoicism of the Greeks in the face of death.

chapter 1

THE BEGINNING OR THE END: IDEAS OF AFTERLIFE

One thing on which most cultures have agreed is that death is not actually the end of anything; there has always been the prospect of a life to come. Or almost always – for there have been odd exceptions to the general rule. Some of America's native peoples, for instance, seem to have had no sense of an existence beyond this on earth. They believed that dead were simply extinguished, as though in a puff of smoke; they might live on in the memory of their loved ones, but they had ceased to be. An austere creed, but – as atheists in our own time will tell us – not necessarily a sad one, for if death holds out no promise, it holds no threat. And if Freud is right in his view that the drive to life is at the same time a drive to death, then the ultimate fulfilment may be found at the very moment of extinction.

NORTHERN AFTERLIVES

Whatever they might have to recommend them, extinction philosophies have been very much minority views in human history. Belief in some sort of afterlife has been all but universal. At its

Left: The ways of the modern world have caught up even with the Inuit; here we see a snow-covered cemetery in Canada's Cambridge Bay.

Right: Odin, greatest of the gods, had ultimate power over life and death in the Viking cosmos.

simplest, the afterlife may be little more than a replication of the mortal world, like the 'Land of the Dead' of ancient Inuit tradition. The burial of the dead in the ground was simply not practical in the ice and permafrost of the far northern regions, and the construction of elaborate tombs would have been an unwarranted drain on the labours of a hunting people constantly battling to survive. So the dead were simply stretched out on the ground (the Eskimos of eastern Asia ritually dismembered their deceased) before being covered over with cairns of stones to keep off scavengers. The Arctic afterlife was similarly straightforward in its conception: the land of the dead was much like that of the living, and only a short walk away for the departing soul. The Inuit funeral was more or less a matter of equipping the dead for this journey, dressing the person in the finest possible parka, with warm boots and mittens – and a little food to eat along the way. (This would actually be eaten by the mourners in what was at once a symbolic act of sharing with the dead and a sensible economy for a people living life on the edge.) The route to the Land of the Dead was clear enough, because the path so closely resembled ones the spirit had used many times in life. On arriving 'home', however, the dead person would be welcomed by the departed of the tribe.

In the longer term, the deceased would get the chance to revisit their loved ones: they were in any case kept 'alive' in their names, which were passed on to newborn babies. As these children grew up, their departed namesakes took a proprietary interest, and returned to the living world to help celebrate the major rites of passage. To begin with, however, the soul had to be encouraged to 'settle in' to a new existence. Returning from the grave site, then, the bereaved relations would ritually 'cut' the trail with a knife or sprinkle ashes so that the dead soul would have to remain on the other side. For a period afterwards, family members were not allowed to use tools.

Hunter-gatherer societies have to travel light, not only in material terms but also in cultural terms – their imaginative lives may be deep and sustaining, but they tend not to be elaborate. The complex cosmologies of the great world religions are the creations of settled societies with spare capacity – designated priesthoods, castes of craft workers and artists, and so forth. Even the Vikings, stereotypically a rough-and-ready warrior people, had a richly complex conception of the universe. The universe, they said, began as the Ginnungagap – a deep crevasse – to the south of which was Muspell, the land of fire. To the north was Niflheim, the icy realm, later to be allocated to the dead as their frigid home. For now, however, its only feature was the great hot spring, Hvergelmir, from which streamed 12 rivers that flowed into the gulf, in whose depths the waters froze, until eventually the Ginnungap had been entirely filled with ice. Warmed by the fires of Muspell, this ice in time yielded moisture, which mixed with the matter of the earth to create a sort of clay. This substance acquired form in the shapes of the great frost giant Ymir and of Audhumla, the Nourisher, the cow whose milk would feed him. With no grass to graze on, she was reduced to licking the ice for her sustenance, and as she did so the first human being took form. Buri, as he is known, was the ultimate progenitor, grandfather of Odin, the greatest of the gods. Ymir himself, meanwhile, created a man and woman from his own sweat. These would be the ancestors of the giants, the gods' eternal enemies. Odin, in fact, was to be the product of both races, born of the coupling

The Arctic afterlife was similarly straightforward in its conception: the land of the dead was much like that of the living, and only a short walk away for the departing soul.

of Buri's son Bor and a female giant. He rose up against Ymir and killed him, and in the gushing blood of the frost giant the rest of the giants drowned – all except for two, one male and one female, who fled far away and established a new realm in what thereafter came to be called Jotunheim, or 'giants' home'.

Odin built the world we know out of Ymir's inert corpse – his blood became the rivers and the seas, his bones the mountain ridges. The world was held up at its four corners by the dwarfs of north, south, east and west. Above arced the vault of the sky, fashioned from the concavity of the frost giant's skull. The fires of Muspell were raided for sparks to serve as stars; the sun and moon were set high in the heavens in their chariots. From the maggots that swarmed in Ymir's decaying flesh, Odin created Dark Elves or dwarfs to mine the darkness beneath the body for gold, in the forbidding underworld that corresponded with the original Niflheim. Odin also made Light Elves, giving them the bright and airy realm of Alfheim. Men and women were sculpted from bits of flotsam cast up along the seashore, and given a realm at the centre of Ymir's body. This Midgard, or 'Middle Earth', was separated from the world around it by a palisade made out of Odin's eyelashes. Odin then created Asgard as a realm for the gods themselves.

As is often the case with complex and ever-developing civilizations, the Nordic myths offer numerous variations on this

Above: The Valkyries swept up the heroic dead and took them off to their eternity in Valhalla.

basic creation myth. The story is of interest, however, not merely in introducing the idea of the underworld but in underlining how fundamental the concept of death was to the concept of creation. Literally so, given that the entire universal edifice was constructed upon and around the dead body of Ymir. As time went on, the notion took hold that there were three different levels of existence, structured vertically: above Midgard was Asgard, below was Niflheim. Reigned over now by Hel, the hideous daughter of the mischievous god Loki, Niflheim was still the realm of the dead – but only for those who had died through natural causes or misadventure. Those who had fallen in the field of battle made their way over Bifrost, a bridge constructed from three interwoven cables of blazing fire, which we now know rather more prosaically as the rainbow. On the far side, high above the earth, lay Valhalla – a vast and majestic hall with 540 doors – where the heroes would spend the rest of eternity in perpetual feasting.

EQUIPPED FOR THE AFTERLIFE

In some cultures, the world of the dead was assumed to be very much like that of the living, with the same customs, the same occupations, the same hierarchies. Hence the tradition, common to many ancient cultures, of leaving 'grave goods' with the dead for use in an after-existence in which they were expected to have substantially the same needs as in the mortal world. These needs may just be creature comforts – a little food or drink, for example. In parts of Madagascar, it is reported, a small radio is sometimes placed in the coffin with the deceased and switched on just before the burial, to keep the occupant entertained in the hereafter. For the earth's elites, however, immediate personal convenience has tended to come second to the maintenance of rank. In Mesopotamia, for example, widely regarded as the 'cradle of civilization', the dead went to their graves equipped according to their social station.

The excavation of Ur began in 1922, a project mounted by the British Museum in cooperation with the University of Pennsylvania. Britain's Leonard Woolley led the 12-year dig, which uncovered much of this early Sumerian metropolis, including the cemetery just outside the city walls. Over 1800 graves were discovered, spanning a 500-year period in the second half of the third millennium BC. By far the majority contained the remains of what must have been ordinary men and women. They were wrapped in reed matting for burial,

Below: Grave goods excavated at Ur have told us much of what we know about life – as well as death – in Mesopotamia.

Above: Backed by his 5000-strong 'Terracotta Army', China's Emperor Shihuangdi could enter the afterlife without fear.

and provided with small offerings of food and drink in earthen pots, presumably to sustain them in the afterlife. A wealthier group had gone to the grave with more valuable items, including alabaster pots and burnished copper mirrors, as well as gold and silver jewellery. The 'Royal Tombs' were not mere graves but proper tombs – built structures, with vaults or domes over the brick-lined underground chambers in which the dead were lain. Here the Kings of Sumer lay surrounded by a spectacular array of priceless treasures: finely crafted vessels in gold and silver; stunning jewellery of exquisitely crafted gold worked in with lapis lazuli, carnelian and other precious stones; an ornamental jar wrought from an ostrich egg; a gaming board of lapis lazuli, bone and seashell; gold-leafed harps and beautifully painted panels, richly ornamented armour and weaponry... the list of wonders went on and on.

A female figure, identified as Queen Puabi, seemed to have occupied a separate tomb alongside that of her unnamed consort: between lay what appeared to have been the mortal remains of their funeral procession. The bullocks that had drawn the dead to their tombs along with their splendid grave-goods had apparently been slaughtered to form a part of the offering – and not just the unfortunate animals but their drivers and their grooms, an honour-guard of warriors and female attendants by the score. Beside them lay cups, from which it is assumed that they took, of their own accord, the poison that killed them. In some cases, however, they appear to have been executed by blows to the head.

We will return to the subject of human sacrifice in a later chapter. For the moment, what seems striking is the perceived requirement for a royal couple to 'keep up appearances' in the next world, to arrive with the same sort of retinue their rank would have demanded in this life. Other civilizations, at other times, found less cruel ways of meeting this need. Egypt's Pharaohs famously went to the tomb with furniture and other luxuries of every kind, some the real thing and others small-scale replicas. There were model servants too – known as *shabtis* – to see to their every need and make sure they wanted for nothing in the Duat, the afterlife. And it was not just a matter of being at the master or mistress's beck and call: just as the Pharaoh conscripted labour from his people, the gods were at liberty to demand work from the dead souls. Hence the importance of having *shabtis:* one Egyptian text describes a distinguished lady entering into a formal

Below: Dressed for death, this Paracas mummy from Peru went to the tomb in layers of rich fabric, a way of 'wearing wealth' and buying status in the world to come.

contractual relationship with hers, so as to be sure that she herself would not have to work for the gods in the world beyond.

A great king would want to cut as impressive a figure in the next life as he had in this. In 206 BC, for example, China's first emperor, Shihuangdi, went into the afterlife backed up by a 'terracotta army': over 5000 life-sized ceramic soldier-statues. All were armed for action – and each, intriguingly, was individualized in his facial features and expression. They were found not far from the emperor's own vast burial mound, laid out with care in three separate pits. The first contained 3107 foot-soldiers, the second 1400 miscellaneous figures, mainly cavalrymen with their horses, but including chariots and charioteers, and a group of crossbowmen. The third pit had the commander of the army, with his chariot, along with his personal bodyguard, his generals and his staff.

Other cultures furnished their departed for the next world in the ways they deemed appropriate. To the earth's elites, it was naturally vital to maintain prestige. The leading caste of the Paracas are a case in point. This people lived in the coastal desert of Peru some 2500 years ago. To begin with, they lowered their dead into bottle-shaped shaft-tombs or cavernas; later they began to build elaborate underground complexes with corridors and courtyards. Invariably, however, they wrapped their dead with the stunning textiles which they specialized in making. Even long after, in Inca times, richly woven and

Below: Extravagant offerings have been found in tombs built for their chieftains by Mississippian communities at sites like this, at Cahokia, Illinois.

embroidered fabrics were much prized in the Andean region, where they would be offered in sacrifice to the gods, and often used as a form of currency. The creations of the Paracas were, however, never to be surpassed in skill or beauty (often, they incorporated exotic imported hummingbird feathers, slivers of spondylus shell or strands of precious metal), but most seem to have been made to be lavished upon the dead. Wealthy men and women would go to the grave with layer after layer of fabric wrapped around them, often with jewellery and other valuables slipped between. In some cases, corpses were found to have been covered in as many as 100 separate layers: these individuals took an estimated 29,000 hours' worth of supremely skilled labour with them to the grave.

The civilization known as the Adena began flourishing in North America at around the same time. Though it was centred on the Ohio Valley, its influence extended through much of what is now the eastern United States. Its dignitaries were characteristically interred in burial mounds: they too were typically accompanied by their treasures. Everything from fabrics and masks to soapstone pipes and beads of shell, as well as mica ornaments of great delicacy. The Adena's successor cultures – the Hopewell (c.100 BC–AD 600) and the Mississippian (c.800–1500) – followed the Adena example in this practice as in so much else. Cahokia, regarded as the capital of a Mississippian state, reached its height some time around the eleventh century. Here, in a platform pyramid raised up out of thousands of tons of earth, one distinguished personage was found lying on a bed of some 20,000 shell-beads. Beside him were piled up 800 stone arrowheads – exchangeable valuables, as well as weapons – and some finely decorated copper and mica plates.

Above: On her passing in the thirteenth century BC, Rameses II's consort, Nefertari, was given a burial 'fit for a queen'.

OF WOMEN AND WAGONS

In many cultures, women of status have been given burials to match those of men: Egypt's Queens Nefertari and Hetepheres I, for example. Dressed to kill in death as in life, Queen Puabi of Ur went to meet her maker adorned from head to foot in breathtaking jewellery. Another royal consort, Fu Hao, a relatively lowly wife of the Chinese Shang ruler Wu Ding, had a tomb packed with bronzes – 440 in all. Almost 600 jade carvings and 7000 cowrie shells were also left with her.

More obviously 'macho' warrior cultures have often shown greater gender acceptance than might be thought, and women frequently attained high status in such societies. Sometime around 300 BC, a Scythian or Sarmatian nomad woman, the 'Amazon Princess of Ipatovo', was placed in a barrow on the open steppe of the north Caucasus. She was petite and slenderly built – which only makes it the more remarkable that the six golden necklets she wore weighed a total of 1.4kg (3lb 2oz). She wore elaborate armlets too, as well as the gold-covered dagger that prompted commentators to describe her as an 'Amazon', a warrior-woman. Two centuries earlier, in Burgundy, eastern France, the 'Princess of Vix' was laid to rest in a barrow, or burial mound. She too entered the world of the dead bedecked with jewellery, and further treasures were heaped up around her, including a bronze krater (a cauldron for serving wine or mead) over 1.5m (5ft) tall. The 'princess' herself lay stretched out on a four-wheeled wagon.

> **The wagon would never have been a status symbol in quite the same way, so we can only guess at why it was included in some graves.**

The interment at Vix was just one of many sumptuous burials carried out by the Celts. Originating in central Europe, the Celts were regarded first with fear and then with condescension by the Greeks and Romans, but their taboo against writing meant they never put their own side of the story. They built an important civilization, though, growing rich on the proceeds of both war and trade, and they were responsible for some of the richest burials ever seen. At Hochdorf, Germany, for example, a mound was excavated in 1977 to reveal a chamber measuring about 4.25 x 5m (14 x 16ft). Along one side of this room was a beautifully engraved bronze couch, upon which lay the body of a chieftain. His neck was surrounded by a torque of beaten gold. He wore armlets, also golden, and around his waist was a gorgeous gold-covered belt. His dagger lay to hand; though made of bronze and iron, this also shimmered with its gold-covered sheath and hilt. His bow and arrows were nearby and, at the foot of his couch, he too had a huge bronze krater, richly ornamented by the Greek craftsman who cast it. On the opposite wall were nine ornately decorated drinking horns.

The other half of the chamber was occupied by a four-wheeled, two-horse wagon, its yoke and harnesses inside, a thing of beauty in itself, with its wondrously fashioned 10-spoke wooden wheels.

The tombs at Hochdorf and Vix both date from around the sixth century BC, but 'wagon burials' of this sort have been found across a wide sweep from Central Europe to the Eurasian steppe, often dating back much earlier. Some 4000 years ago, warriors of the Indo-Iranian Andronovo culture were often buried with their battle chariots; this civilization seems to have invented the spoke-wheeled chariot, and these vehicles would have been their owners' pride and joy. The wagon would never have been a status symbol in quite the same way, so we can only guess at why it was included in some graves. Was it simply because it had carried the deceased to his or her tomb, and had thus somehow been consecrated? The Greek historian Herodotus, intriguingly, describes dead Scythian warriors being driven about in the backs of wagons for 40 days, 'visiting', as it were, their families and friends and being welcomed like living guests, even offered food. Or, of course, the wagon could have been placed in the barrow, or *kurgan,* to give the departed a means of making the journey to the next world.

INTO THE UNKNOWN

The idea of death as a journey has been shared by many cultures. The journey to the Greek underworld is not dwelt upon much in the mythology, but mention is made of the fact that the soul was conducted to the underworld by Hermes, the messenger of the gods, while the crossing of the River Acheron (sometimes the Styx) aboard the boat of Charon is of obvious symbolic importance. For some cultures, clearly, the journey matters as an ordeal, a trial of some kind; for others, it appears to be the crossing of some crucial threshold that really counts. The traversing of the blazing Bifrost bridge by the souls of dead Vikings would seem to be a journey of this latter sort. Ship-burials, however, perhaps suggest that death is a quest, a voyage. Famous ship-burials took place beside Oslo Fjord, at Oseberg and Gokstad, Norway.

The tenth-century Iranian traveller, Ibn Fadlan, describes the funeral rites offered for a local chieftain on the Volga. This was a region whose Slavic natives had embraced the ways of the Swedish Vikings, who passed up- and downriver between the Baltic and Kievan Rus. To his surprise, Fadlan says, the ruler's ship was hauled ashore, and amidst elaborate ceremonies he was placed aboard, in a little pavilion amidships; a favoured concubine was ritually raped by six of his men, then killed in sacrifice and placed beside him.

Then the people came forward with sticks and firewood. Each one carried a stick, the end of which he had set fire to and which he threw in amongst the wood. The wood caught fire, and then the ship, the pavilion, the man, the slave-girl and all it contained. A dreadful wind arose and the flames leapt higher and blazed fiercely… It took scarcely an hour for the ship, the firewood, the slave-girl and her master to be burnt to ashes, and then dust of ashes.

Below: Ship-shape – literally – in death, this grave at Gottlands Lan in Sweden was designed to carry its occupant off to the afterlife.

The Pilgrim's Progrefs. Pt 2d

The Pilgrim's Progrefs.

Deftruction.

Start-ts.

THE
Pilgrim's Progrefs.
FROM
THIS WORLD
TO
That which is to come.
The Second Part.
Delivered under the Similitude of a
DREAM,
Wherein is fet forth
The manner of the fetting out of *Chri-*
stian's Wife and Children, their
Dangerous JOURNEY,
AND
Safe Arrival at the Defired Country.

By *JOHN BUNYAN,*

I have ufed Similitudes, Hof. 12. 10.

LONDON,
Printed for *Nathaniel Ponder* at the *Peacock,*
in the *Poultry,* near the Church, 1684.

**Above: The all but
universal instinct to see
life – and death – as a
journey is exemplified in
literature by allegories
like John Bunyan's
Pilgrim's Progress (1678).**

They built something like a round hillock over the ship, which they had pulled out of the water, and placed in the middle of it a large piece of birch on which they wrote the name of the man and the name of the King of the Rus. Then they left.

Such extravagant obsequies can't have been routine: a ship was enormously valuable, and would not have been disposed of lightly. This was an outrageous example of what we would now call 'conspicuous consumption'. But there were less spectacular ways of acknowledging the notion of death as a sea-voyage, as we see from the many humbler graves whose headstones were shaped like ships, or simply decorated pictorially with ship motifs. And at the Viking cemetery at Lindholm Høje, in northern Jutland, we see smaller standing stones set out in patterns around the graves. While several shapes can be discerned, including rectangles and circles, many plainly represent the outline plan of a ship's hull.

It made sense for a seafaring people to see death's journey as a voyage across an ocean, but more landlocked cultures thought in terms of a long cross-country trek. For North America's Plains Indians, the horse was as important as the ship was to the Viking. When a warrior of the Lakota Sioux died, his favourite horse would often be sacrificed alongside him to carry him to the land of the dead, which was thought to lie far to the south. As recently as the nineteenth century, people in the mountains of the Czech Republic were buried in boots, to be ready for the weary hike to come. Some Slavic traditions saw the road to heaven as following the brilliant bend of the rainbow; in others, dead souls had to make their way across the heaving backs of thunderclouds. At any moment, angry spirits might erupt from inside these tumultuous billows (or, in some versions, bands of ferocious Tartars).

If the afterlife was often envisioned as being in some way a reflection of this one (whether as blissful idealization or dismal parody), death's journey was obviously imagined as a metaphorical version of life itself. We are accustomed to the schematization of existence as an arduous and testing journey from allegorical works of literature, like John Bunyan's *Pilgrim's Progress* (1678) or, for that matter, the *Divine Comedy* (1308–21) of Dante, in which the poet is taken on a tour to view the destinies of the dead. So it is no surprise to find the way to the afterlife being barred by challenges of one sort or another. Again, Slavic tradition is a fruitful source. Many storytellers described the journey of the dead souls along the starry course of the Milky Way, running the gauntlet of four giant

Below: In the *Divine Comedy* of Dante, the poet made his own journey through the realms of death.

mowers who stood ready to scythe them down before they could reach the sanctuary of heaven. In pre-Christian Lithuania, wild animals were cremated alongside the human dead so that the departed might make use of their sharp claws. These would be needed in the event of death, to assist the soul in its ascent of the sheer mountain of polished metal or glass that had to be scaled to reach salvation. Even in recent times, Russian peasants often carried rings and amulets as good-luck charms, containing owl talons or the clippings of their own fingernails. To commence its journey, the soul had first to make the climb out of the grave itself, so wooden ladders or knotted ropes were often buried with the dead. This tradition endured into the modern age, in the little ladder-shaped loaves of bread that were placed in the coffin beside the corpse.

For the Slavs of Bulgaria, however, the soul took flight as a butterfly or bird, lingering to witness its own obsequies, before flitting off towards the land of death. The butterfly, beautiful but fleeting, is emblematic everywhere of the delicacy of life, but the Bulgars pursued this symbolism further. Other Slavic cultures saw the stars as souls. Every time a child was born, the story had it, a new one twinkled in the firmament, but, by the same token, every meteor marked another death. As would be expected, given the imagery they used, the old Slavs did not believe in an underworld as such. Their land of the dead was a distant country, known variously as Peklo, Nava or Rai. All went here, regardless of their conduct in life; only gradually, in the Christian era, did a distinction creep in between a heaven-like Rai and Peklo, now a place of punishment.

Thousands of miles away, in what is now Mexico, the Aztecs believed that the dead had to make the journey to the land of Mictlan in the deserts of the north. This was a terribly hard and hazardous trek: souls had to traverse rugged mountain ranges and a rushing river before finding their way down a narrow ravine between clashing crags. Then they had to scale the steep and slippery slopes of a mountain of obsidian – volcanic glass – braving winds that could flay the skin right off their faces. They had to brave monsters, more rivers and mountains, and finally fight it out with demon guards before they made their way into the presence of Mictlantecuhtli and Mictlancihuatl, the king and queen of the underworld.

It was a dreadful journey, for which there was really no preparing the dead, but even so their grieving relatives did what they could. People were buried with food and blankets and spare clothing, and their dogs were often buried or burned beside them to guide them along the way. Dogs were held in great affection as pets in Aztec society as in the present day, but they had a symbolic importance beyond their value as companions. The great god Quetzalcoatl, most familiar in his form as the 'plumed serpent', had another identity as the dog Xolotl (in some accounts he was a twin brother, or an unrelated companion-god). It was in this guise (or in this god's company) that Quetzalcoatl had made his own journey to Mictlan at the world's beginning, bringing back the bones of the first ancestors, from which he then fashioned the human race.

Gifts were also left with the dead, as offerings to Mictlantecuhtli. The hope was that he might be appeased, his approval bought. To no avail, for the god was implacable and the heroic journey was to have no great prize at its conclusion for anyone. First, in his rage, Mictlantecuhtli tore the physical body into pieces, thus releasing the essential soul from its earthly form. That was basically the end: the

It was a dreadful journey, for which there was really no preparing the dead, but even so their grieving relatives did what they could.

Left: Mictlantecuhtli, the Mesoamerican god of death, bears a fittingly ferocious countenance in this breastplate found at Monte Alban, in Oaxaca, Mexico.

soul lived on – or endured – through a perpetuity of darkness and cold, and well-nigh unremitting tedium. The only relief came in the annual festivities of the day of the dead, when they were allowed to make brief return visits to the land of the living.

The obsidian mountain in the Mesoamerican myth had associations with the god of night and sorcery, Tezcatlipoca, but the similarity with the glass mountain in the Slavic story is intriguing nonetheless. Such coincidences are, however, less strange than they may appear, even though the two cultures could hardly have been farther removed from one another, geographically or historically. To study any of the great universals is to be reminded alternately of the enormous diversity and the deep continuities of human life and culture.

No journey is more momentous than that made by a baby when it is born. Or more traumatic, it might be said. Snatched from the security of its mother's womb, the infant is forced to face the tribulations of the world. And yet, without making this journey, it would never know the joys and satisfactions that life has

Below: The ideas of womb and tomb come together in the gentle curves and swelling mounds of the Chinese cemetery in Malacca, Malaysia.

to offer. Several civilizations have regarded death in just this way. Anthropologists Richard Huntington and Peter Metcalf found a striking example of this viewpoint in their studies of the Bara of Madagascar. They made a point of passing the dead person through to the world of the ancestors headfirst, as though in birth, and saying: 'Here is your grandchild, born here. Do not push him away, even from here.'

From the perspective of the reader raised in a Western school of self-conscious individualism, life may seem linear, with the womb and tomb at opposite ends. But many cultures naturally see existence in terms of cycles of death and rebirth – even the Judaeo-Christian tradition does at its more abstract theological level. Many of the tombs in Malacca's Bukit China (Chinese cemetery) give this association physical form, the tomb entrance opening up vagina-like beneath the swelling convexity of the grassy hillside. Other traditions may make the link less obvious, but it is not hard to find at least a hint at the idea of human fecundity in the gravid roundedness of any barrow, or burial mound.

In some cultures, the rites of death may be seen as simply another stage in a series of rites of passage, akin to the initiation ceremony through which the youth passes into manhood. This would imply that death is the transition into another, more grown-up stage of life, a view that makes complete sense in those cultures in which the ancestors are believed to endure, a background presence among the living. The Dowayo of Cameroon see death as analogous to coming of age, and so its rites echo those of circumcision – the body is trussed up in the same posture as that of a boy being circumcised. Such thinking seems logical enough when it is recalled that for the Dowayo, as for so many other cultures in West Africa and elsewhere, the manhood rituals endured by the living youth are seen as representing his figurative dying and rebirth.

ENDURING FAME

Anthropologists sometimes talk of the distinction between the 'shame culture' and the 'guilt culture'. Many early societies fell into the former category. Courage was the ultimate virtue, glory the great prize, and the warrior feared the contempt of his comrades far more than any still small inward voice. Even in the Christianized Anglo-Saxon England of the tenth century, the author of the heroic poem, 'The Seafarer', declared:

> Indeed hotter for me are
> The joys of the Lord
> Than this dead life
> Fleeting on the land.
> I do not believe
> That the riches of the world
> Will stand forever...

A mature, and recognizably Christian outlook – yet how does the poet believe we are to transcend this vale of tears?

> And so it is for each man
> The praise of the living,

In some cultures, the rites of death may be seen as simply another stage in a series of rites of passage, akin to the initiation ceremony through which the youth passes into manhood.

Of those who speak afterwards,
That is the best epitaph,
That he should work
Before he must be gone
Bravery in the world.

Here we see an idea of eternal life merging with the old warrior ideal in which the aim is to attain lasting fame and to be spoken of well, celebrated in both song and story. It is important to appreciate the strength of the hold such an ethic would have had on a great many societies in history when we seek to understand their views of death.

The great dolmens of prehistory, the burial mounds of America's Adena, the Pharaohs' pyramids, were not just houses for the dead, or receptacles for treasure, but monuments. Visible from afar, they proclaimed to all who saw them their occupants' importance. Raised up in the Yamato Period, between about AD 300 and 600, the *kofun* of Japan are a case in point. Often known as 'keyhole mounds' from their distinctive shape in bird's eye view, these could be quite enormous in their size. The one built for the Emperor Nintonku, who died in 427, for example, reaches a height of 35m (115ft). Approximately 480m (1575ft) in length, it covers an area of 185 hectares (458 acres) and is surrounded by three concentric moats. Japanese archaeologist Umehara Sueji estimates that its construction would have occupied a thousand labourers over a period of well over four years.

This scale was partly the point, of course. By its sheer size, such an earthwork announced the significance of the personage in whose name all this soil had been shifted. But the *kofun* spoke in more subtle ways too. Typically, these mounds were stuck like porcupines with a wide variety of talismanic *haniwa* – cylindrical ceramic sculptures that stood upright in the ground, facing outward to the world at large. These were cunningly fashioned in the form of animals (from fish and chickens to horses and wild boar) and also into people, beautifully executed in loving detail. Often these are recognizable as farmers, falconers, soldiers, stable-boys, musicians, dancers and courtesans. These may have been intended as a 'staff' to attend the dead ruler in his afterlife, but it is thought more likely that they advertised the glories of his mortal reign. They may also have provided detailed information about the dead man's property and interests, but this must remain a matter of conjecture. At the centre of the *kofun* – the most sacred part – *haniwa* typically took the shape of houses (implying safe sanctuary for the spirit?) and birds and boats, which presumably conducted the soul to its final home.

Real life begins when that burden is laid down and the unencumbered soul is free to join the ancestors.

SACRED PLACES

When the African-American abolitionist whose former masters had given her the name Isabella Baumfree finally got to choose her own name, she called herself 'Sojourner Truth'. 'Truth', because that was what she spoke, or rather what she said God spoke through her; 'Sojourner', because she was just a visitor on earth. Evangelical Christians have often taken very seriously the belief that their mortal existence is just a preparation for the life that matters, the one that they will lead with their God in the hereafter.

Left: *Haniwa* in their hundreds adorned Japanese *kofun* burial mounds, but their meaning remains unclear. Did this house denote worldly real estate or a home for the departed soul?

Such a view would sit well with the beliefs of the animists of Madagascar, for whom the breathing, suffering body is just a burden. Real life begins when that burden is laid down and the unencumbered soul is free to join the ancestors. Typically, the dead are housed in tombs of stone, laboriously and often expensively constructed; rude wooden shelters are deemed sufficient for the living. Standing in the earth around these tombs are richly carved wooden posts

called *aloalos,* often topped with a design representing the dead person's occupation. These too are labours of love: the bereaved family lavishes care and expense upon them, but ultimately they are simply left to fade and rot. They are not intended as monuments or memorials, though, for the dead are held to be alive, not just in the memory but in fact. Rather, they mark the connection between the two worlds. That connection is further underlined by the hundreds of *fady,* rules and taboos associated with the ancestors, governing everything from dietary matters to agricultural methods.

There is evidence to suggest that the burial mounds of many cultures served a similar purpose, as nodes or contact-points, sacred places at which the worlds of the dead and the living came together. It is hard to know whether what were already regarded as sacred sites were chosen for burials or whether it was the presence of a burial that conferred sanctity, but it is clear that mounds and barrows were invested with mystic significance. The most immediate consequence of this, perhaps, was their use for successive burials. Archaeologists investigating the *kurgan* at Ipatovo have identified 13 different phases of use, dating from the fourth millennium BC to the second millennium AD.

THE DEAD REVISITED

It is believed, however, that burial sites became centres for other ritual activities. In their book *Inside the Neolithic Mind* (2005), researchers David Lewis-Williams and David Pearce argue that what we call megalithic 'tombs' were really something rather more: 'They were also places where the dead were revisited and where people maintained long-term relations with them: they were religious and social foci' (p.179). More even than this, they suggest provocatively, that the burial sites were monuments to thought, embodiments of the ideas by which these supposedly primitive people organized their world. In their orientation; in the causeways and kerbstones over which they were approached; in their external shape and their internal layout, the distribution of their different chambers; in the presence or absence of niches, marks or more elaborate inscriptions – in all these aspects, the Neolithic peoples mapped out an aesthetic and a sense of order. How did the builders comprehend their universe, or their own place in it? How did the heavens relate to the earth? Did they see death as a fixed condition or as a passage, a process, a state of change? And what sort of life – and afterlife – did they believe in? All the answers might potentially be found recorded in such constructions. And, since cosmology reflects consciousness, we might ultimately even be able to attain some sort of understanding of the minds that made them – not just what they thought but how, neurologically, they thought.

An exciting enterprise indeed, though Lewis-Williams and Pearce acknowledge the difficulty in knowing exactly how such monuments should be 'read'. This is true enough: scholars have studied many hundreds of these sites in exhaustive detail, but how are they to know which, out of all these details, are the telling ones? Even if it is necessarily inconclusive, however, their theory remains exciting, giving us a sense of just how much may be at stake in the study of burial practices in general, how much they may show us about the ways that different peoples saw their place in the world and in their cosmos. An idea of its afterlife helps to demonstrate where a civilization sees itself in the bigger scheme, where it situates itself philosophically in the here and now.

Left: 'Chosen women', set to weave prestigious textiles for the Inca king, the *Aqllakuna* retained their special status in the tomb.

ANCIENT FUNERARY RITES

If every civilization has its own distinctive
way of life, it also has its own way of death.
The dead, after all, have to be disposed of by
the living. The funerary practices of any
given society are an aspect of its wider ritual
life, and are deeply embedded in its cultural
traditions. Death has its public, political aspects: if
the individual has fears of mortality and hopes for
the afterlife, society and the state have something
invested in the idea of death and resurrection. When
a man or woman dies, their sons and daughters
survive, and, though death comes daily, the life of
the community goes on. Such are the cycles by
which a society endures.

Several civilizations in the ancient world placed
the rituals of death at the very heart of public life.
The most celebrated example of this is found in
Egypt. The Pyramids, the Valley of the Kings, the
tomb of Tutankhamun, death masks and mummies –
the paraphernalia of Pharaonic death has captured
the modern imagination. Most of us are upbeat in
our enthusiasm for these macabre reminders of
antique mortality. How, though, did the Egyptians
themselves see death?

**Left: Antiquity's most instantly recognizable relic,
Tutankhamun's death-mask means that, for us at least,
the Egyptians lived on via their rituals of death.**

Right: Osiris was the Egyptian god of fertility and also death: with his crook and flail, he was part-planter of new life and part-grim reaper.

EGYPTIAN WAYS OF DEATH

When we refer to 'ancient Egypt', we are talking about a complex society that developed under different ruling dynasties. Through its various political crises and environmental catastrophes, it endured for a period of more than 3000 years – a longer time, in other words, than has yet to elapse since the works of Homer were composed, or the city of Rome was founded by the Latin tribes.

It is worth remembering that Ancient Egypt was a region hemmed in by desert on either side and bordered by mountains to the south, meaning that it was to some extent naturally inward-looking and self-contained. With the rhythms of the Nile floods imposing a regular routine on economic production over many centuries, there was every reason for a continuity in cultural life. From a later perspective, constants can certainly be traced, recognizable themes that seem distinctively 'Egyptian'.

Despite the importance attached to death, it would be wrong to assume that the Egyptians were especially morbid or depressive – their view of mortality was by no means all doom and gloom. The Lord of the Underworld, Osiris, was the god of fertility as well, and as such stood for fresh starts as well as endings. For Egypt was fundamentally an agrarian society, and the planting of seeds in the soil provided a positive analogy for burial, with the promise of rebirth. This perspective worked in the opposite direction too: the burial of the dead, and the trust in their resurrection, helped bolster the belief that the Nile mud would give forth life again. 'I am the plant of life,' read one text often included in the coffins of the dead: 'I allow the people to live and the gods to be divine... I live as corn, the life of the living... my love is in the sky, the earth, the water and the fields.' Egyptian views of life and death reflected and reinforced one another to such a degree that there is little point in viewing them separately.

Left: Recognizable by his distinctive snout, Seth, the son and avenger of Osiris, does battle with his uncle Horus for authority in Egypt.

So, if death took place in the midst of life, life was present even in the tomb, whether symbolically or in some cases literally. The idea of regeneration was given physical reality by the 'Osiris Bed', which was a feature of tombs in the New Kingdom (1550–1070 BC; one was found with Tutankhamun). A wooden frame, shaped like the figure of the god, it was filled with soil and seed, which germinated after the tomb had been sealed. The 'corn mummy', as it is also known, was a living, growing emblem of the resurrection for which the Pharaoh hoped; it also reproduced the rebirth of the god himself, killed in legend by his jealous brother Seth. His widow Isis gathered up the dismembered limbs, which his murderer had scattered throughout the land, then revived him and brought him to arousal. The subsequent sexual union resulted in the birth of a son, Horus, who grew up to avenge his father, killing Seth. Osiris also became associated with the dying sun, which sets each night to rise in the morning, and dwindles away in winter to return after the solstice.

SPRITUAL HOMES

Not surprisingly, perhaps, the Egyptian afterlife, or *Duat,* was much like this one. The land of the dead lay beyond the western horizon (where, of course, the sun went when it 'died'). The dead Pharaoh was seen as sailing across the sky on a reed raft or wooden boat, steered by a sinister-looking helmsman who always looked backwards. Sometimes known as the 'Field of Reeds', the other world actually amounted to an alter-Egypt: a great river ran through an open and level plain, which was ringed around by mountains. Osiris ruled here like a Pharaoh (and, of course, the converse held: the Pharaoh served as a sort of Osiris in the land of the living).

Like Egypt's earthly ruler, Osiris conscripted labourers from the dead to cultivate his crops and bring in the harvest, though some individuals brought *shabtis* (*see* Chapter 1) so that they themselves would be at leisure. Or they would come armed with spells, which would enable them to evade these duties. One Egyptian spell explicitly offered to teach a person 'How not to decay or have to labour in the afterlife'. Brief texts on scraps of papyrus were included with a body, often bound into the bandaging of the mummy. More than a thousand different 'coffin texts' are known, including everything from prayers to Osiris, through directions to the kingdom of the dead, to lucky charms to ward off attack by demons. Some were inscribed on other items, including scarab-shaped amulets: these would stop the individual's heart from offering evidence against him or her. Much of this wisdom was later collected into the *Book of the Dead,* a text that ran to some 200 chapters. In some accounts, when the soul's work for the day was done (or from dawn to dusk, if it was served by *shabtis*), there were indeed rewards to be had in the kingdom of the dead. Then the spirit was free for feasting and lovemaking. Other myths are bleaker, however, describing souls waiting out the ages in the chilly darkness.

The Egyptian soul had a number of different aspects, including everything from the name of the individual to his or her shadow. Purely as a life-principle or energy, the soul was called the *ka* – this was the force that distinguished the living body from the corpse. (When, so the story went, the creator-god Khnum first moulded men and women from the Nile mud, he shaped their *kas* as well, their spiritual equivalents.)

So if death took place in the midst of life, life was present even in the tomb, whether symbolically or in some cases literally.

The *ba* was the personalized spirit of the individual, which made them what they were. The *akh* has been described as the 'spirit of immortality', and it resulted from the union of the *ka* and *ba* after death. It was the highest spiritual state any human being could attain, and every Egyptian aspired to achieve it (iconographically, it was represented by the crested ibis). If the right offerings were not made, or the right prayers said or enchantments uttered, this union did not take place, and the body was said to have died a second time. This was the soul that made the final journey to the land of the dead; the others remained with the mummy in the tomb. A new *ba* was formed, and this was believed to be able to make brief visits back to the land of the living, behaving much like the 'ghost' of our modern understanding.

Below: This scene from the Egyptian afterlife comes from the papyrus *Book of the Dead* found in the tomb of Neferrenpet, a scribe of Rameses II who died around 1250 BC.

In predynastic times – in other words, before they had come together into their Pharaonic state – the people of Egypt buried their dead in the ground in graves. They laid them huddled up in what was presumably meant to be a foetal position, ready for rebirth in the world beyond. By 2686 BC, with the dawn of the era known by scholars as the Old Kingdom, they were laid out flat, facing east to greet the rising sun.

The first pyramid was built soon after, at Saqqara, across the river from the royal capital at Memphis. Egyptian rulers had already had splendid tombs built for themselves at Abydos, stone-built 'palaces' in which they could spend the afterlife. But Imhotep, vizier to Djoser, a Pharaoh of the Third Dynasty, wanted something more special, more spectacular, for his master. Hence the creation of the first pyramid. Stepped in construction, it stood 60m (370ft) tall. It looks like a staircase to the sky, suggesting that when Djoser died, these steps would be the

Below: Re-Harakhty, or Horus, sails his solar boat across the sky – life's journey towards death was seen as analogous to this daily voyage.

means by which Djoser progressed to the afterlife. An esplanade, enclosed by an imposing wall, was laid out before this vast monument: the pyramid would provide an impressive backdrop for royal appearances and parades. With hindsight, it can be seen that this complex, though ostensibly designed to serve as a tomb, was primarily conceived to promote the Pharaoh during his mortal reign.

A more complex cult of the dead emerged in the course of the reigns that followed, as the Pharaoh became identified as a living god. He was the representative on earth of Re, the god of the sun, and when he died he crossed the sky to the country of dead, where he took on the identity of Osiris. A pyramid text from this period makes the idea of the 'stairway to heaven' explicit: 'The king goes to his double ... a ladder is set up for him that he may ascend on it.' However, as time went on, and the sun-cult gathered momentum and imperial architects became more ambitious, this sort of 'step pyramid' gave way to smooth-sided structures. Their angled edges formed straight lines that reminded onlookers of the rays of the sun. The idea of the ladder was giving way to one of a more effortless apotheosis. 'I have laid down for myself those rays of yours', says the Pharaoh to the sun-god in another inscription, 'as a stairway under my feet on which I will ascend.'

The first of these 'true' pyramids took shape in the reign of Sneferu (2613–2589 BC), when the steps of an earlier construction were filled in. He went on to build two more pyramids at Dahshur. But it was his son Khufu who was to build the biggest and most famous of the pyramids: the Great Pyramid at Giza covered over 5.3 hectares (13 acres) and rose 146m (480ft) into the sky. It was carefully aligned with the points of the compass and its mass concealed a cunning system of internal passages and chambers, so that Khufu's corpse could be housed in comfort and safety. Yet its most striking feature was its sheer size: until the construction of the Eiffel Tower at the end of the nineteenth century, this was to be the tallest construction in the world. It still dominates the encroaching apartment blocks of suburban Cairo. Brilliant architects masterminded construction and skilled stonemasons did the finer work, but the building of the pyramids was as much a miracle of organization as of engineering. The Pharaoh's scribes administered an elaborate corvée system by which farmers and peasants contributed their labour as a form of tax, working in large gangs under the direction of experienced overseers. The bulk of the heavy work – quarrying and hauling blocks of stone – was done during the flood season, when nothing could be achieved on the land. There was no shortage of work to do, as Giza's Great Pyramid contains over two million blocks of limestone, many weighing as much as 15 tonnes (14.7 tons).

The pyramids were just the most obvious features of what were really extensive funeral complexes, with temples where the dead would be received, and paved procession ways across which they would be carried to their resting-place. The Old Kingdom was the golden age of pyramid building; those of the Middle Kingdom (c.2055–1650 BC) were 'jerry-built' by comparison – stone or mud-brick rubble was piled up and then clad with solid slabs, which often sagged or collapsed after a time. But doing the job properly involved a commitment daunting even for a Pharaoh, and the Great Pyramid is thought to have tied up 20,000 workers for 20 years or more.

They laid them huddled up in what was presumably meant to be a foetal position, ready for rebirth in the world beyond.

This consideration, along with the difficulty of guarding the pyramids against grave-robbers, seems to have prompted the switch to underground tombs in the era of the New Kingdom (c.1550–1069 BC). By this time, the imperial capital had been moved from Memphis to Thebes, some 600km (370 miles) upriver. It was Amenhotep who first had a secret tomb dug out of the rock of a remote valley on the other side of the Nile from his seat of power. There was symbolism in this siting: the land of the living was in the east; the other world lay in the west, towards the setting sun. Over the centuries, a complex was constructed in an area that became known as the Valley of Kings, its underground chambers and passages a symbolic replication of the underworld. At the mouth of the valley were the 'mortuary temples', each one custom-built to handle the body of a different Pharaoh.

MAKING A MUMMY

Much needed to be done, of course, before a body could be laid in its tomb, for the Egyptians had a horror of decay. This was more than mere fastidiousness. The belief had taken root that if the body did not remain intact, the soul would not endure. In pre-dynastic times, bodies were laid directly in the searing sand of the desert, and naturally mummified, but the Pharaohs were now paying the price for their grandiosity. Removed from the dry desert earth and placed in a pyramid or mausoleum, bodies broke down, as they would in any other setting. The Pharaohs were most reluctant to forgo their magnificent monuments, and so the embalmer's art came into being.

Egyptian embalming was at once a skilled technique and a mystic ritual whose secrets were passed on down the generations through dynasties of practioners. In the absence of written Egyptian accounts, we are forced to fall back on the testimony of ancient foreign historians like Herodotus and Diodorus Siculus, who visited Egypt at at time when the Pharaohs had been in decline for several centuries. Even so, what they say appears to be borne out by chemical analysis. They described what they saw in detail, perhaps in horrified fascination. 'This is their procedure', notes Herodotus:

> ...for the most perfect style of embalming. First of all, they draw out the brain through the nostrils using an iron hook. When they have extracted all that they can, they wash out the remnants with an infusion of drugs. Then, using a sharp obsidian stone, they make a cut along the flank. Through this they extract the whole contents of the abdomen. The abdomen is then cleaned, rinsed with palm wine and rinsed again with powdered spices but not frankincense, and stitched up. And when they have done this, they heap the body with natron [a dehydrating salt] for seventy days, but no longer, and so the mummy is made. After the seventy days are over, they wash the body and wrap it from head to toe in the finest linen bandages coated with resin.

Diodorus Siculus describes an alternative method for treating the body:

> One of them inserts his hand through the wound in the body into the breast and takes out everything except the kidneys and the heart. Another man cleans each of the entrails, washing them with palm wine and with incense. Finally, having

Egyptian embalming was at once a skilled technique and a mystic ritual whose secrets were passed on down the generations through dynasties of practitioners.

washed the whole corpse, they first diligently treat it with cedar oil and other things for thirty days, and then with myrrh, cinnamon and spices.

In the great days of Egyptian embalming, the long hook that pulled out the brain would have been made of bronze, not iron, but in other respects these accounts seem quite convincing. The organs removed, the lungs, the liver, the stomach and the intestines were placed in special containers called 'canopic jars'. These had ornamental stoppers, generally taking the forms of the four sons of Horus: a human, a falcon, a jackal and a baboon. Before it could be bandaged,

Above: As shown in this nineteenth-century impression, the ancient Egyptian embalmment was part-technical treatment and part religious ritual.

the body would have to be 'stuffed', the abdominal cavity filled with bundled cloth or sawdust. The linen bandages were applied a layer at a time – good luck charms were left between each one. Many layers would be applied – up to 368 square metres (3960 square feet) in all. The binding process typically took 15 days. Once it was complete, the finished mummy was wrapped up in a simple shroud. A death-mask, painted with loving care, was then placed over the head to give the mummy a human face – a great Pharaoh might have a death-mask made of gold and precious stones. The mummy was then placed inside a wooden coffin that was roughly human-shaped and painted inside and out with decorative motifs and magic charms. Again, a particularly wealthy ruler might be buried, in a 'nest' of coffins place one inside another like Russian dolls.

Only when all these preparations had been made in the most meticulous detail was it possible to think of the funeral itself. This was as grand an occasion as might be imagined, given that the Egyptian state had made the Pharaonic death-cult not just the mainstay of its ritual life but the engine of its economy. The funeral procession would set out from Thebes in solemn ceremony, attended by priests and dignitaries, family members and other mourners. A splendid funeral feast was carried behind by a train of servants as the Pharaoh's mummified body was dragged down to the river on a wooden sledge. There it was transferred to a boat to make the crossing, before being unloaded on to another sledge. On the body's arrival at the threshold of its final resting place, ritual dances were performed, and prayers or spells were chanted. These were directed specifically at the different parts of the body, which had to be prepared for their later reawakening. This stage culminated in the 'Opening of the Mouth': the mouth was touched and incantations offered so that the soul would be able to speak and breathe in the afterlife.

Only when these formalities were over could the body be placed in its stone sarcophagus, and consigned to the tomb to await rebirth. Around it were grave goods – often in considerable abundance. These included food and drink to sustain the soul before its rebirth; along with cooked meat and bread,

Left: Nefertari lived to a ripe old age, giving her husband, Rameses II, time to build her the most sumptuously painted tomb in the 'Valley of Queens'.

Below: Osiris sits in judgment over the suppliant soul in this illustration from an Egyptian Book of the Dead.

53

Tutankhamun's tomb contained over 100 baskets of fruit and 40 jars of wine. There were *shabtis,* model attendants, often equipped for particular operations: ploughmen with teams of oxen, agricultural labourers and lady's maids.

Discovered in 1925, the burial chamber of Queen Hetepheres I – wife to the Pharaoh Sneferu, the pyramid builder – included everything she could have needed to make her comfortable. Her bed, her headrest and a pair of armchairs were there, as was a litter on which she could be carried: this was inscribed with her regal titles in gold and ebony. There was also a jewellery box, covered in gold and containing 20 silver bracelets. These were beautifully inlaid with butterfly forms in lapis lazuli, carnelian and turquoise. The queen's gorgeously decorated curtain box was there, though its contents were gone, presumably stolen around the time of her burial. The tomb of Nefertari, Rameses II's queen, was systematically looted in ancient times, so was empty when rediscovered in 1904, but it still took the breath away with its stunningly painted plasterwork. Beneath a deep-blue ceiling painted with golden stars, pictures and hieroglyphs depict the late queen's journey to the afterlife under the protection of the gods. We see her as a mummy and as a woman playing *senet,* a sacred board game; we see her answering riddles posed by the gatekeepers of the kingdom of the dead. She is able to answer them thanks to the presence of painted passages from the Book of the Dead. In the innermost heart of the tomb, she was interred in a sarcophagus of pink granite: 'the womb from which the queen [would] eventually be reborn,' observes Egyptologist Joyce A. Tyldesley.

GREATER IN DEATH THAN IN LIFE?

Scholars are still attempting to come to terms with the treasures of Tutankhamun unearthed by archaeologist Howard Carter in 1922. It was on 26 November that he broke a hole through the sealed door:

> At first I could see nothing, the hot air escaping from the chamber causing the candle flame to flicker, but presently, as my eyes grew accustomed to the light, details of the room within emerged slowly from the mist, strange animals, statues and gold – everywhere the glint of gold.

The room beyond was crammed with everything from furniture to flowers, from exquisite vases and precious caskets to chariot parts. There were statues of gods and goddesses, smaller *shabti* figures, and a life-sized effigy of the king himself. There were gilded beds, an ornate headrest and an inlaid throne. The king's courtiers had thought of everything, for there were humbler offerings here, including firelighting equipment and supplies of food. There was a *senet* set in this tomb too – the Egyptians seem to have seen the playing of this board game as a compelling metaphor for the progress of the soul towards the afterlife.

And this was just the anteroom. Only after these goods had been systematically cleared over a period of weeks was Carter able to penetrate the actual burial chamber. A system of pulleys was used to lift the lid of the massive stone sarcophagus. Inside lay what turned out to be a 'nest' of three coffins. The innermost was of solid gold, over 2.5cm (1in) thick. When its lid was raised, the mummified body of the young ruler was exposed to human eyes for the first time in over 3000 years:

Left: Tutankhamun took his decorated throne with him to the tomb, so he might continue to reign – under Osiris – in the afterlife.

Above: To modern eyes, the torments of Tartarus have a faintly absurd, almost festive air.

Before us, occupying the whole of the interior of the golden coffin, was an impressive, neat and carefully made mummy, over which had been poured anointing unguents… In contradistinction to the general dark and sombre effect, due to these unguents, was a brilliant, one might say magnificent, burnished gold mask or similitude of the king, covering his head and shoulders, which, like the feet, had been intentionally avoided when using the unguents.

Thanks to this stupendous death-mask, Tutankhamun has become the most familiar Pharaoh to our own age, though he hardly set the Nile alight in his own lifetime. In recent years, controversy has raged over whether he was assassinated in what is known to have been a period of dynastic struggle. He was just 14 years old when he ascended the throne, and barely into his twenties when he died. He was quickly forgotten, a fact that may have helped to preserve his tomb. Debris from other building projects in the Valley of Kings, or silt swept over the site by floodwaters, may have helped to conceal its entrance from subsequent searchers. Though Carter found evidence that robbers had been there before him, this seems to have happened at a very early stage, and whatever may have been taken, priceless treasures had been left.

GREEKS BEYOND THE GRAVE

Among their many contributions to the modern world, the Greeks have given us a marvellous mythology, including some of the most colourful stories of Western culture. Among them are the tales of Tartarus, the very pit of dank despair, far beneath even the gloomy halls of Hades. Here, we are told, those who have offended the gods spend eternity in torment. The Titans, for example, are imprisoned here: the children of Uranus, first father of the heavens, and of Gaia, mother of the earth, they were overthrown by Zeus and forced to make way for his Olympian deities. Tartarus is coeval with creation – all that remains of the primordial chaos – which makes its symbolic geography significant. It implies an eternal order underpinned by the fear of damnation, an ever-present warning that existence is a serious business.

Left: Sisyphus, for his sins, was condemned to push a massive boulder up a slope; each time he neared the top, it rolled back down – and so on, for all eternity.

Extravagant as Classical mythology is, it has been notoriously difficult to be certain what it actually meant to its originating culture.

That said, the myths of Tartarus often seem as festive as they are frightening, like the torments of Ixion on his wheel. The King of the Lapiths had cruelly killed his own father-in-law, but Zeus showed him mercy, even inviting him to visit on Olympus. Ixion repaid this kindness by seeking to seduce Zeus's queen, Hera, and it was for this crime that he was cast down into the abyss. His punishment was to be fixed to a fiery wheel that would spin for ever. Tantalus was another one damned for his abuses of hospitality. He was Zeus' own son, born of the nymph Plouto. Invited to dine with his father, he stole some ambrosia – the heavenly food of the gods – and took it back to earth to share with his family and friends. He was no more agreeable as a host than he had been as a guest, serving up his own son Pelops, cut up and cooked, as a meal for the gods. He was condemned to spend eternity with his own hunger unsatisfied, forced to stand in a pool of water beneath a tree whose branches hung low with fruit. Every time he reached up to pick one, the branch drew away and he was cheated; every time he bent down to drink, the waters parted and he was left thirsty. He thus became the type for the person whose desires are cheated just in that moment when they are apparently being realized – and gave us our modern word 'tantalize'.

Sisyphus, too, was a violator of codes of hospitality that must have been deep-rooted in Greek culture. He took travellers into his home and then stole from them. He was also a trickster, several times deceiving the gods themselves, a humiliation that was not to be borne. His punishment in Tartarus was to push a boulder up a hill. Just as he seemed to be succeeding, it would slip from his hands and roll down again. Like Tantalus, he is a type that suffers everlasting 'so near, yet so far' frustration, but his struggle also suggests the endless rising and setting of the sun. Ixion's wheel has obvious solar associations, of course. In their different ways, all these stories can be seen as musings on the idea of eternity and just what it may mean.

What they cannot be seen as is credible warnings. Their tone is one of grotesque whimsy; if they hint at the hell of Hieronymus Bosch, they remind us more of his playful ingenuity than his feverish fears. They are, moreover, wholly exceptional in the canon of Greek myths – we have no sense that mortal men and women were encouraged to dread such destinies for themselves. The impression that these experiences lay outside the norm was arguably underlined in heroic literature by the protagonist's *katabasis*, his journey to the underworld. Ulysses makes his descent in Book 11 of Homer's *Odyssey,* and sees for himself the punishments of Sisyphus, Tantalus and others. Similar descents were to be de rigueur in later epics: in Virgil's *Aeneid* and much later, in medieval times, in Dante's *Inferno.* Long before this, however, indeed as early as 405 BC, when Aristophanes' play *The Frogs* was performed, such stories and images were being parodied by comic writers.

Extravagant as classical mythology is, it has been notoriously difficult to be certain what it actually meant to its originating culture. Did the Greeks and Romans 'believe' in their gods in the way in which a modern Christian or Muslim might believe in their creator? Did they live and breathe Zeus and Venus the way a Buddhist does the transience of all things? In fact, as far as we can tell from the sources, the destiny of the dead was one of a drab greyness very much at odds with the colour and vibrancy of Greek mythology in general.

Some stories hint at the conspicuously virtuous gaining their reward in the 'Elysian Fields', but these are as exceptional as the tales of Tartarus. The inclusion of coins with the dead, apparently as fare for the ferryman Charon, suggests that some credence was given to the tradition that the dead had to cross the River Acheron or Styx. Beyond that, though, the myths are vague. Many educated Greeks appear to have seen death as a journey into the unknown – a metaphysical problem, it might be said. Socrates, condemned to die for his supposed 'corruption' of Athenian youth, was duly philosophical about his fate:

> Depending on how we look at it, we may hold on to the hope that death is a sort of bonus. For what happens to us at death is one of two things. Either the dead person just ceases to be, losing all senses in a sea of nothingness; or else, as many people believe, it is a change, a migration of the soul towards another place.
>
> Well, if death is simply the end of our sense, then it is like a long dreamless sleep, and therefore a sweet prospect. If you can recall that rare night when you

Below: This woman at Paestum, a Greek settlement in southern Italy, may well have been genuinely missed, but these lamentations were more about her rank and status.

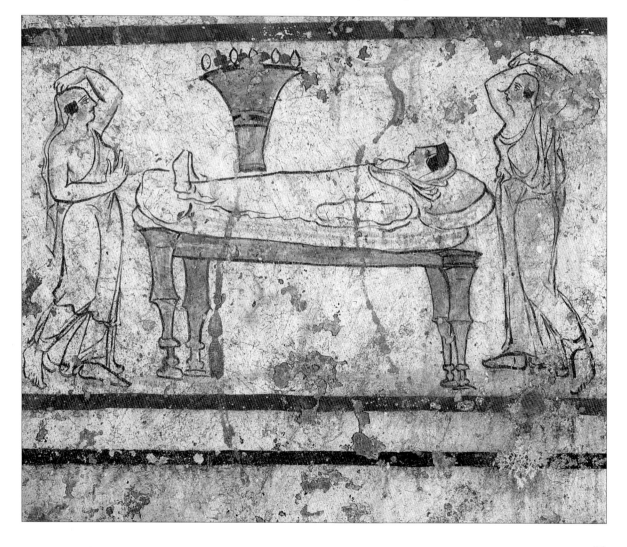

slept so deeply that you were undisturbed by dreaming – can you remember anything more pleasant? … If that is how death is, then I for one am looking forward to it – for then eternity will be like nothing more than a single night.

But suppose that death is, indeed, a journey to another place. Suppose the destination is as commonly imagined, and contains the spirits of all who have died. I ask you – what prospect matches that? Who would not want to travel to that other world? … Think how much it would be worth, to have conversations with Orpheus and Musaeus, with Hesiod and Homer!

Whether the average Greek was able to face death so calmly seems doubtful, on the whole – indeed, Socrates appears to be arguing against what he considers to be the widespread fear of dying. Such evidence as we have, however, suggests that what people dreaded most was the loss of life, its joys and pleasures, rather than the prospect of punishment. 'I'd rather be a day-labourer on earth,' says Homer's Achilles, 'working for a man of little property than lord of all the hosts of the dead.'

The Greeks took their funerary rituals seriously because, while they may not have had anything much to look forward to in the afterlife, they were haunted by the fear of having to remain on earth as ghosts. A corpse that went unburied – or uncremated – could not make the journey to the underworld, which meant that it could never hope to find its final rest. Rituals varied from city to city and over time, but the basic process was pretty much constant, typically being divided into three stages.

First there was the laying-out of the corpse, the *prothesis,* as it was called. The body was washed, anointed with oil, covered with a shroud and exhibited on a bier – sometimes for several days. The deceased would then be visited by friends and relations, neighbours and, for a public figure, by members of the wider community. Next came the 'carrying out', or *ekphora:* the body was placed in a cart and carried in procession to the cemetery, often accompanied by musicians. Family members wept and tore their clothes, or slapped their heads in histrionic shows of grief – our word 'histrionic' actually originates from this practice.

Simple grave goods would have been left with the dead – offerings of food and drink were a feature of burials all the way through into late Classical times.

In the world's first democratic societies, public image counted for much, so the perception of popularity was much prized. Every citizen, said Plato in the fourth century BC, aspired to be 'sent off in great style'. Hence the ostentation with which the dead were mourned – the Greeks thought nothing of paying professional mourners. At last, the corpse was laid to rest in its grave, or placed on a pyre and burned. The ashes were then, generally, placed in a jar or urn and buried. Graves were placed in family plots so that the departed could be with their loved ones. Libations of wine, oil or even blood, were poured into the ground.

By Classical times at least, Greek graves were simple trenches in the ground; earlier Aegean cultures had sometimes had more imposing tombs. In Mycenaean times (c.1600–1500 BC), ordinary people were placed in the ground or in natural caves or cavities cut from rocky hillsides. Simple grave goods would have been left with the dead – offerings of food and drink were a feature of burials all the way through into late Classical times. These graves would probably have been marked by memorials of painted wood. Great warriors were interred in deep,

Left: Cyrus the Great made the construction of his own tomb the centre of an imperial cult that would be continued by his Persian successors for generations.

stone-lined shafts. Grave goods were again included, ranging from simple offerings of food and drink to golden treasures. *Stelae* – carved stones – marked such graves; these might well show a battle or a hunting scene to suggest the noble pursuits of the deceased. Later on in the Mycenaean period, beehive-shaped tombs, or *tholos*, were built for important individuals. These could be up to 14.5m (47ft) in diameter and 13.2m (43ft) high.

It seems to make sense that the democratic age would favour more modest graves, and certainly there was nothing like the *tholos* of the Mycenaean era. The Athenian government actually introduced laws to limit the construction of elaborate tombs – though the fact that they had to implies, of course, that some of its citizens were tempted. For the most part, graves were simple, though care and expense might be lavished on the *stele* as a mark of status – these were often sumptuously carved.

Left: Alexander the Great discovers the body of Darius III after his assassination: the tombs of Persia's emperors became important religious centres.

PERSIAN PRACTICES

The great enemies of the Greeks were the Achaemenid Persians, whose customs must indeed have seemed profoundly alien to their European foes. In recent years, scholars have been coming to a clearer estimation of the astonishing achievements of this great Asian empire, displaying a new scepticism towards the 'black propaganda' of the Greeks. That said, Greek commentators remain among the most important sources we have on the ancient Persians, whose own historical record has been largely lost.

While all the evidence tends to suggest that the Achaemenid emperors were conspicuously enlightened rulers, they were certainly not democrats by instinct. Like the Egyptian Pharaohs, they made their funerary traditions a part of the institutional structure of the state. The desire to mystify the imperial person and to create a monument to his power may be the reason for the Achaemenids' rejection of what was already an established tradition for remains to be left outside for scavengers. According to Herodotus, 'the dead bodies of Persians are not buried before they have been mangled by bird or dog.'

Their rulers were to make an exception for themselves. On his death in 529 BC, the founder of the Achaemenid Dynasty, Cyrus I 'the Great', was buried in a monumental tomb in his capital, Pasargadae. Above the door, we are told by Plutarch, was an inscription in Aramaic, which reads oddly to us now – half arrogant, half unassuming:

> O man, whosoever thou art and whencesoever thou comest, for I know that thou wilt come, I am Cyrus, and I won for the Persians their empire. Do not, therefore, begrudge me this little earth which covers my body.

Inside, however, all was majesty and pomp. Another Greek chronicler, Arrian, spoke to some of the Greeks who violated the sanctity of this tomb after Alexander the Great overthrew the Persian Empire in 333 BC.

> In the chamber lay a golden sarcophagus, in which Cyrus' body had been buried; a couch stood by its side with feet of wrought gold; a Babylonian tapestry served as a coverlet and purple rugs as a carpet. There was placed upon it a sleeved mantle and other garments of Babylonian workmanship. According to Aristobulus, Median trousers and robes dyed blue lay there, some dark, some of other varying shades, with necklaces, scimitars and earrings of stones set in gold, and a table stood there.

Darius I (reigned 521–486 BC) began the building of a new capital at Persepolis, and had his tomb cut into the rock of a nearby outcrop at Naqsh-i Rustam. Its frontage echoed the façade of Darius' imperial palace, underlining the continuity

Above: The necropoleis of the Etruscans, like this one at Cerveteri, were laid out as veritable 'cities of the dead'.

between his life and death. Darius himself was depicted above the door, on a throne held aloft by his devoted subjects. An inscription offers praises to Ahura Mazda, the Zoroastrian deity, lord of light, and records the conquests of Darius the Great. Within were a series of chambers, filled with treasure, presumably, before Alexander came this way. The emperor himself would have lain in the innermost recesses of the tomb. Further tombs were built by Darius' successors, seven in all, though that of Darius III was left unfinished in what was to become known as the 'Hill of Kings'.

ETRUSCAN AND ROMAN RITES

Far to the west, meanwhile, central Italy had seen the rise and fall of the Etruscans, who by the fourth century BC were eclipsed by the power of Rome. Little is known of their living civilization, in fact, or of their history in their heyday, since the only real record we have is to be found in their cemeteries. Archaeologists have discovered what appear to be the remains of settlements, often on hilltops and apparently built in wood and mud-brick, but the dwellings of the dead were constructed far more durably. (They were, of course, expecting to occupy them far longer.)

The most famous Etruscan necropolis is at Banditaccia, near Cerveteri. The tombs here are laid out like the buildings of city. They line the 'streets' in their hundreds, built both above and below ground level, their underground passages and chambers carved out of the solid rock. But stone blocks were also used to create circular superstructures overhead with dome-shaped roofs, some more than 40m (130ft) in diameter. These were covered over with earth, and then became overgrown. The largest of these tumuli have up to four different tomb-complexes beneath them; smaller, squarer structures stand above single tombs, humbler 'homes' to the dead of poorer families.

Yet the biggest, most prestigious tombs are veritable mansions of mortality, with ornamental pillars, doorways and even furniture cut into the rock. The dead were laid out as though put to bed on couch-shaped shelves of rock – their heads sometimes resting on stone pillows – or were placed in sarcophagi of stone or terracotta. Some of these have figures of their occupants carved on their lids. On one famous example, a couple reclines as though dining together. In some of the grandest tombs, the impression of being in a living interior is enhanced by the décor, richly painted or adorned with carved-stone or stucco reliefs. Scenes of feasting are a favourite – perhaps these show the funerary banquet – but other subjects include everything from lions to stormy seas. The finest examples of Etruscan wall-painting are, however, to be found at another necropolis, at Tarquinia, where scenes from everyday life, myth and ritual were executed in astonishing detail and stunning beauty. These marvels of ancient art complete the impression the Etruscan cemeteries give us of a civilization for whom the illustrious dead were expected to spend eternity in some style.

In funerary practices, as in so much else, the Romans followed the lead of the Greeks. Their conception of the afterlife was substantially the same. So too were their burial rites, but they seem to have felt more strongly than the Greeks that death was something to be kept at a distance. The Roman dead were banished safely beyond the realm of the living – quite literally: cemeteries were established outside the city limits. Archaeologists Jon Coulston and Hazel Dodge have described how, as the Roman metropolis expanded, a 'bow-wave of cemeteries flowed ahead'. Often tombs were sited beside the main roads in and out of town, and many are still to be seen along the Appian Way.

But the dead did continue to exercise a role in the life of the family and the wider community. Whilst the unburied dead or lemures roamed the world as ghosts, unable to find a sanctuary, those who had received the right obsequies comprised a collective deity, the *di manes* (from *di*, meaning 'gods' and *manes*, 'ancestral spirits'). Roman gravestones were often inscribed 'D.M.', meaning *dis manibus* – for the manes. Important though they were, they were entirely dependent upon their mortal relations, their immortality enduring only as long as the sacred rites went on being observed. Every year, between 13 and 21 February, they were honoured at the festival of Parentalia, their relatives going to the graveyard to make offerings of grain and wine or oil. These would be poured

The Roman dead were banished safely beyond the realm of the living – quite literally: cemeteries were established outside the city limits.

onto the grave; some tombs, in the cemetery at Ostia, the port of Rome, had special tubes running from the surface, so that libations could be channelled into the very presence of the dead. This was a cheerful celebration with something of the flavour of a family picnic about it, but was followed by the altogether darker rites of Feralia. These addressed mortality in its more forbidding aspects and set out to appease the infernal spirits. The Parentalia found a form of 'closure' in the feast of Carista as attention shifted back on to the living. Any outstanding quarrels had to be made up now and the family had to get together, ready to face whatever challenges might lie ahead.

As time went on, wealthy Romans vied with one another in commissioning ever more spectacular tombs, culminating in those of the Augustus and Hadrian. These mausoleums were never to be surpassed, chiefly because Rome's greatest magnates were, no doubt sensibly, reluctant to give the impression of attempting to upstage their emperors. Indeed, the trend in the first century AD was towards less pretentious, even austere, tombs. At the same time, however, members of a moderately prosperous 'middle class' were moving up-market, joining funerary collegia or clubs and buying shares in stone- and brick-built mausoleums. Scores – sometimes hundreds, and in a few cases even thousands – of urns of cremation ash could be housed in these, each with its own individual cavity in the interior walls. Lined up in their tiers and serried rows, these resembled the niches of a Roman dovecote, or *columbarium* – the name by which these facilities are now known. Underground burial complexes or catacombs were also built: these were organized along very much the same lines.

MASKS OF MEMORY

Historical convention finds it convenient to think in terms of distinct, and always separate, civilizations: the Egyptians, the Greeks, the Romans, and so forth. Such divisions make sense, up to a certain point, but the mummy portraits found at Fayyum, Egypt, remind us that the realities of life – or death – are less easy to categorize.

These portraits, painted on wooden boards, seem strikingly modern in their sensibility, accustomed as we are to the stiff and stylized forms of so much ancient art. Instead, meticulously realistic and utterly human, they gaze out at us, their expressions clear and open, engaging us emotionally across some 2000 years. In the same way, it is believed, they would have helped to maintain the human connection between their dead subjects and the living families who commissioned them in the first century AD. Scholars suggest that these portrait-masks were probably placed over the heads of mummified bodies, which were then kept upright in the entrance halls of houses. Here they would have remained, to be met and greeted each day as their surviving relations came and went: only after many months might they have been buried.

The paintings were produced at a time when Egypt had, for three centuries and more, been under foreign domination, first that of the Greek Ptolemies, and then the rule of Roman Empire. Quite how it happened we may never really know, but the attitudes and traditions of these different cultures intermingled and interacted to create these masterpieces. In the end, all these ancient civilizations shared, both with one another and with ourselves, a compelling need to find a meaning in the fact of death.

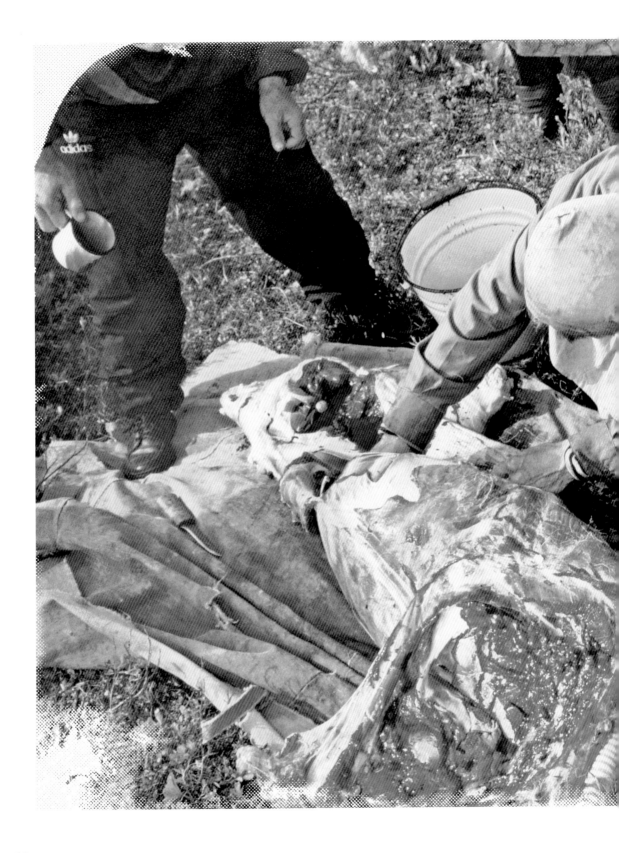

chapter 3

DEATH AND JUDGMENT

In the cinematic cliché, as the bullet bites or the body hurtles groundward, the events of the life that is ending flash before us in fast review. Much is made of our duty to remember the dead, but death itself may be seen as a moment of recollection, the conclusion that confers shape and meaning on the narrative as a whole. Sophocles' remark (*see* Introduction) that we should consider no man happy till his life is finally over, is founded in this idea of death as a moment of reckoning, of taking stock.

Anthropologist Piers Vitebsky describes a funeral among the Eveny, reindeer-herding nomads of Siberia's Arctic north. In certain respects, it is every bit as exotic and 'ethnic' as might be expected. A favoured reindeer is sacrificed in honour of the departed, its meat shared between the mourners and the deceased, choice morsels being set aside to be placed upon the grave. Its bones, picked clean, are placed in a box, having first been carefully counted to make sure that all are there, for if any are

Left: Siberian nomads prepare the reindeer sacrifice that will secure the departed safe passage to the afterlife.

Inset: A fourteenth century illustration by Hartman Schedel showing a Dance of death.

missing, the beast will be lame and unable to carry the soul on its last migration. The head and antlers are displayed atop this box, which is left beside the grave. The whole process is a prehistoric tradition enduring intact into our own age.

Well, not completely intact. Indeed, on closer inspection we find that nothing here is intact, either symbolically or literally:

> The grave was a palimpsest of all the doctrines that had touched the Eveny during the last 300 years, clustering around the mystery of death to offer competing certainties. The bland mottoes on the plastic wreaths served as neutral captions for a montage of shamanist offerings, wooden Orthodox crosses, and Soviet stars snipped out of red-painted sheet metal…
>
> To visit a recent grave was to stand in an eerie silence of shattered objects, each symbolically 'killed' so that it could pass into the next world. Vodka bottles were smashed, cigarettes snapped in two, wooden sledge-runners cracked, tin bathtubs punctured. On a child's grave, toys were ripped and dolls mutilated. The grave was a portal from this world to the next which sucked in not only the dead but also everything that the living brought as offerings, and even – if they looked backward – the living themselves.

To the modern imagination, the words 'death' and 'judgment' seem to go together, but we have already seen that this has not always been the case.

This last comment is why, as they leave the graveside, the relations take special care to stare fixedly forward, 'for fear that the dead person would interpret the most fleeting glance, the slightest betrayal of longing, as invitation to take the mourner with them'. Backward glances, in some sense, 'belong' to the dead.

The world has moved on, for the Eveny as for everyone else; and time waits for no man – not even for nomads. At the individual level too, time changes as childhood gives way to adulthood and – after a long, full life, it is hoped – the soul departs in death. But if life may obviously be seen as a progression, a moving forward, its ending involves a retrospection, a looking-back. There is disagreement among the Eveny about what the afterlife will be like, Vitebsky finds, but from somewhere in their kaleidoscope of creeds, a consensus has emerged about the journey there:

> For the first forty days the dead person would fly around and revisit all the places they had ever been on earth, 'to complete their work here before flying to heaven'.

For their 'work' to be concluded, it seems, it has to be checked over, repeated, rehearsed; only in death is this sort of examination possible.

IN THE FINAL ANALYSIS

To the modern imagination, the words 'death' and 'judgment' seem to go together, but we have already seen that this has not always been the case. Among many Australian Aboriginal tribes, as among the Inuit and other Arctic hunters, the world beyond is seen as a replica – or even an actual continuation – of this one. Before Buddhism introduced the notion of death and reincarnation, Japanese Shinto envisaged an afterlife in which the dead were divided – as they had been in life – by social rank. Their underworld, called Yomi, was a dark and dismal place, but in its social geography it was just like the earth above. The Greeks had Tartarus for a few egregious enemies of the gods and, in some stories, versions of

heaven in the Elysian Fields or the 'Blessed Isles'. For ordinary men and women, however, death held no greater threat (or promise) than that of extinction, or an eternity in a bleak but unjudgmental Hades. Egyptian tradition did to some extent envisage the life of the departed being assessed: in several reliefs, the jackal-headed Anubis, god of mummification, is shown holding up a hand-scale in which he weighs the heart of the deceased. But we have little sense of this judgment being 'followed through' into an afterlife of reward or punishment; there is no real Egyptian intimation of a heaven or hell.

Writing in the first century AD, the Chinese philosopher Wang Chong quotes the *Shan-hai-Ching* (Book of the Mountains and Oceans, now lost) on how his countrymen saw the journey to the life to come:

> The mountain Tu-shuo arises from the centre of the blue (eastern) ocean. On it stands a huge peach tree that twists itself over an area of 3000 li. An opening of its branches in the northeast is called kuei-men, 'the gate of the spirits of the dead'. There, the ten thousand spirits of the dead go in and out. Above them are two gods named Shen-t'u and Yu-lu. It is their responsibility to inspect the ten thousand spirits of the dead. They seize the evil and harmful, tie them with ropes and throw them for the tigers to eat.

Wang Chong was, it has to be said, a 'freethinker', deriding many of his contemporaries' views as superstition. He scoffed, for example, at the idea of ghosts (something in which his generation believed implicitly) and produced what he plainly saw as a definitive put-down:

> People say that spirits are the souls of dead men. That being the case, spirits should always appear naked, for surely it is not contended that clothes have souls as well as men.

In early centuries at least, Judaism was remarkably vague about the destination of the dead, who seem, indeed, to have been out of sight and out of mind.

Be that as it may, we have no real reason to doubt Wang Chong's account of the Shan-hai-Ching with its anticipation of a final – and ferocious – judgment.

Modern 'Western' religious and ethical beliefs are generally assumed to owe their origins to the Judaeo-Christian tradition, and nine times out of ten that assumption is justified. It is liable to mislead us here, however. The Old Testament may be rich in fire and brimstone, but its descriptions of the afterlife are less fierce than might be supposed. In early centuries, at least, Judaism was remarkably vague about the destination of the dead, who seem, indeed, to have been out of sight and out of mind. 'I am as the man that hath no strength,' says the Psalmist, 'Free among the dead, like the slain that lie in the grave, whom thou rememberest no more: and they are cut off from thy hand.' Not just gone but forgotten; and not just departed but deliberately discarded: Sheol, the underworld, was a place of abandonment. The Biblical Gehenna was, even more emphatically, a version of oblivion. First mentioned in the Book of Joshua, it was named after a tip outside Jerusalem where rubbish – including bodies of outcasts – had been burned.

To find a likely source for Christianity's concern with eschatology (the 'Four Last Things': Death, Judgment, Heaven and Hell), we have to look not to Judaism but to Zoroastrianism. This ancient Persian religion was widely disparaged by the monotheistic religions as a primitive paganism, a form of fire-worship, but nothing could have been further from the truth. The Indo-Aryan ancestors may well have worshipped fire, but they certainly had every reason to revere it. Fire gave them warmth and light; it protected them from wild beasts and cooked their food; it was mysterious and, in early times at any rate, hard to make. Under Zoroastrianism, however, this sanctity became symbolic: fire was the source of light, enlightenment and purification.

The change came as early as 1200 BC (though some scholars suggest a date as much as 5000 years earlier) when Zarathustra, or Zoroaster, first propounded his

Left: Yama – or, in Persia, Yima – was Lord of Death. He held the entire universe and its cycles in the form of an ever-turning wheel.

Above: Today, as for so many centuries, Iran's Zoroastrians revere fire as a symbol of spiritual purification.

beliefs. As the official doctrine of the Persian Empire, Zoroastrianism was widely disseminated throughout Western Asia (and, after conquests in the region by Alexander the Great and by the Romans, its influence filtered further west). The god of the Zoroastrian universe was Ahura Mazda, father of order and light, but he was from the very beginning locked in conflict with Angra Mainu, originator of darkness, disorder and destruction. The war between the two is eternal, and takes place at every level of existence, from the cosmos as a whole to the individual conscience. Zoroastrians also saw everything in terms of this dualistic schema, from the creation of the world to the moral problems of everyday life. All of us, Zarathustra thought, faced a lifelong and profoundly personal struggle so that we might let light prevail over the dark forces fighting for possession of our souls.

The Central Asian nomads from whom the ruling castes of both India and Iran were to spring saw the hereafter as being organized very much along earthly lines. While noblemen could expect their lives of rank and privilege to continue beyond the grave in a heavenly paradise, the poor (and all women) went to an undifferentiating realm of the dead. This was ruled over by a Lord of Death, associated with the setting sun, who became the Vedic deity Yama or the Persian Yima (or, later, Jamshid). Such an arrangement was quite alien to the oppositionist thinking of the Zoroastrians, for whom it seemed self-evident that virtue and wickedness would have divergent destinies. While all would ultimately be saved when Ahura Mazda gained his final victory over Angra Mainu at the universe's end, the good and bad would go their separate ways until then. After death, the soul stayed close to the body it had left, reluctant to leave the mortal world behind. It remained on hand for three days and nights, meditating on the life just lived: on the first night, it reflected on its words; on the second, its thoughts; on the third, its deeds. Even in death, darkness and light continued contesting the soul's ownership, as demons tried to drag it down into the underworld. But the virtuous spirit was buoyed up by its own goodness and by the prayers of those who mourned it. On the fourth day, the soul set off for the afterlife. To reach the world beyond, it had to cross the Bridge of Chinvat. This might be translated as the 'Bridge of Reckoning' (the word *chinvat* originally meant 'clerk', or 'accountant'); here the soul was audited, the good and evil in it assessed. This was the responsibility of the Yazata ('adorable ones'): Mithra, Sraosha and Rashnu weighed the spirit in their scales to establish whether it deserved to be saved or damned.

The good were taken under the protection of a beautiful maiden, who led them across the bridge to the House of Song, a paradise of light. The bad, on the other hand, were met by a stinking, freezing hideous hag, her features wizened by age and ravaged by disease, the personification of their own corrupted souls. For the virtuous, the bridge was a broad and easy thoroughfare; for the wicked, a hazardous climb across a rocky ridge, from which sooner or later they plunged into the pit of demons far below. This was explicitly a place of punishment, but in other respects resembled earlier underworlds in being a place of dark and dismal bleakness. Fire was, of course, overwhelmingly positive in its associations in the Zoroastrian scheme, so the flames of later Christian infernos would have been out of place. But this sink of despair differed too in being a place of segregation, in which the souls were kept apart. This was to be a feature not only of Zoroastrianism but of Eastern Christian traditions, as Alice K. Turner has observed in *The History of Hell*. 'In Byzantine art the damned are shown in isolated "boxes," a device not seen in the West, where Hell is characteristically chaotic and crowded.'

The judgment of the Yazata was scrupulously precise – a single sin either way could, quite literally, tip the scales. But there were some individuals in whose lives the good and evil exactly balanced. They were sent to a third place to wait out their eternity, assaulted alternately by cold and heat. Hamestagan, as it was called, is often equated with the later Christian concept of purgatory, but this comparison does not entirely hold. Indeed, given that Zoroastrians expected existence to culminate in Ahura Mazda's triumph, in the destruction of evil and thus in the redemption of the good in everyone, their hell was itself arguably a purgatory, a place of finite – and ultimately purifying – torment.

JUDGMENT, JEWS AND CHRISTIANS

Much the same might be said of the Jewish view of damnation, which Rabbinical tradition has generally agreed is over after a maximum of a year. It has been suggested that the Jews came into contact with Zoroastrian ideas during the Babylonian Captivity of the sixth century BC, and this may well have helped

While noblemen could expect their lives of rank and privilege to continue beyond the grave in a heavenly paradise, the poor (and all women) went to an undifferentiating realm of the dead.

colour Jewish attitudes to death and judgment. Just when and how it happened must remain in doubt. It does seem very likely, however, that the Persian creed exercised its influence on Judaism as it developed. Certainly, by the first century BC, the old, undifferentiated Sheol was giving way to a twofold vision of an afterlife, in which the wicked were damned while the good went to the bosom of Abraham. If this distinction seems clear-cut, what it meant more specifically was not spelled out. As far as we can see, salvation was a state of blissful union with the creator; damnation was the deprivation of that happiness for a limited period. Beyond that, there was no attempt to endow the underworld with a topography – it was much like the Sheol or Gehenna of before.

The idea of hell's fire does have its precedents in Jewish thought: the Book of Isaiah ends with a warning of the fate in store for the 'carcasses' of 'the men that have transgressed against men'. The prophet states: 'Their worm shall not die and their fire shall not be quenched, and they shall be a loathsome sight to all flesh' (LXVI, 24). While obviously drawing on the associations of the historical Gehenna as a dump in which dead bodies were burned as a means of refuse-disposal, Isaiah also clearly sees fire as a form of punishment here. Christ himself harks back to this text when, in the Gospel of Mark (IX, 45) he speaks of 'eternal damnation ... in the fire that shall never be quenched.' For the most part, the gospels have little to tell us about the afterlife. Even Matthew who, as Alice K.

Below: The Church Fathers wrestled with the problem that, interpreted rigorously, Christ's teaching seemed to exclude even patriarchs like Abraham from salvation.

Turner points out, goes out of his way to underline the torments in store for the wicked, does not give us great detail. It is, however, to him that we owe familiar images of hell as a place of 'wailing and gnashing of teeth' (XIII, 402, 50) and as the 'outer darkness' (XXV, 46).

The evidence is that the early Christians were similarly inexact about the prospects for the world to come, though fervent in their hope that they were going to an everlasting life with God. They certainly do not appear to have dwelt too much on the realms to which the damned were to be banished. The prevailing view seems to have been the old Jewish one, with damnation a matter of exclusion, of abandonment to oblivion. This perspective would have made sense to those brought up in a Greco-Roman cultural world, with its drear and gloomy Hades. What the Christian sought was the life everlasting; not to attain that was damnation enough, hence St Paul's pronouncement that 'the wages of sin is death'. Paul's attitude is especially interesting, since he is so often held up as the first puritan, an implacably stern moralist, the man who took a creed of forgiveness and made it vengefully severe. Even he, however, seems to have seen a joyful salvation as the reward for the good Christian; its deprivation a sufficient punishment for the sinful.

The *poena damni*, or 'pain of loss', remains an item of Catholic doctrine to this day; so too, though, does the *poena sensus*, 'pain of sense'. Hell in this view is a real place, the pit in which the damned will spend their eternity along with Lucifer and his demons – those rebellious angels who had been cast out from heaven with him. Many modern theologians feel uncomfortable with the idea of this sort of hell, believing that what was meant metaphorically has been taken literally. Estrangement from God; exclusion from joy; the absence of eternal bliss: these are negative, even abstract concepts, whereas readers respond to the positive, the concrete. Faced with this problem, it may be argued, the writers of the Bible looked round for an imagery that would reinforce their warnings: they did not believe they were mapping out an actual hereafter. There is much to recommend this view. The Bible is a written text – and an extraordinarily rich and complex one, at that – so it is open to all manner of different interpretations, with different emphases. But what might be called the 'exclusion theory' has been marginalized in the popular tradition precisely because people do respond more immediately to an infernal vision of flames and sufferings than to one of 'mere' loss.

The medieval Church was at once the product and perpetuator of a society in which learning was the preserve of an elite, who instructed the unlettered masses in what they should believe. From the first, we can see a dichotomy emerging between a hell of exclusion for the educated and a (literally) sensational one for the vulgar masses. This was no straightforward division: hell with its fires and demons was official doctrine, and all would have believed in it, but it remains the case that, to some extent at least, the higher up the hierarchy one looks, the more 'philosophical' hell's conception has tended to be. 'We must not ask where hell is,' wrote St Chrysostom, 'but how we are to escape it.' This sounds suspiciously close to ducking a quite reasonable question.

St Augustine, however, was never one to evade an issue, and in his *De Civitate Dei* ('The City of God', 426) he plunged right in with a palpably physical description:

The evidence is that the early Christians were similarly inexact about the prospects for the world to come, though fervent in their hope that they were going to an everlasting life with God.

> Hell, which is also called a lake of fire and brimstone, will be material fire, and will torment the bodies of the damned, whether men or devils – the solid bodies of the one, and the aerial bodies of the other. Or, if only men have bodies as well as souls, still the evil spirits, even without bodies, will be so connected to the fires as to receive pain without bestowing life. One fire certainly shall be the lot of both.

The description appalls us now, partly because it strikes us as so footling – why expend such intellectual energy on whether spirits could experience physical pain, or whether the human damned and devils were to endure separate damnations? And, of course, dwelling almost lovingly as it does on the torments of the damned, it seems to associate righteousness with sadism. Context is all, of course: Augustine was responding to a current in the Church of his time that was, he felt, too confident in man's ability to ensure his own salvation. A complacent Christendom had to be jolted into fear, he felt.

Yet the impulse to map out the world beyond did not just stem from the need to make things clear to the ignorant masses on the one hand or to terrify them into obedience on the other. A genuine debate had arisen amongst the Church's leading clerics as they wrestled with some of the implications of the Christian scheme. The medieval Church was well aware of just how problematic its various positions were on this most vexed of questions. A new scholarly subject developed, that of 'eschatology'. This was the study of the 'Four Last Things' – Death, Judgment, Heaven and Hell – and there was to be no more contentious field in Christian theology.

LIMBO, ITS RISE AND FALL

Never having been baptized, they could never know the bliss of being with God – but then, in their ignorance, they would not miss that ultimate felicity.

Take, for example, the eternity's damnation to which Christ had apparently condemned the most virtuous figures of antiquity...and the most innocent babes: if King Herod had ordered the murder of the Holy Innocents, a strict reading of the scriptures implied that the God of Christ would consign dead infants to perdition.

At first glance, the gospel message was simple and joyful: Christ had redeemed the world with his 'New Covenant', and now all could freely choose the path of salvation. Of course, it was fair enough that those who spurned the proffered redemption should be damned, but what was to become of those who had never had the chance? John's gospel is explicit: 'Unless a man be born again of water and the Holy Ghost, he cannot enter into the kingdom of God' (III, 5). Where did this leave those who had never been offered the gift of baptism? In a truly rigorous interpretation, these included even Abraham, the patriarch – beloved though he obviously was of God – as well as observant Jews and sundry 'virtuous heathens'. And then there were those – far more numerous in the medieval world than in today's advanced industrialized societies – who died as babies, before they could be baptized. How could they be damned to hell, simply because their lives had slipped away untimely? The need for some alternate state was obvious.

Hence the idea of Limbo, a realm in which those who had never had the opportunity to receive God's grace could live out their eternity. Never having been baptized, they could never know the bliss of being with God – but then, in their ignorance, they would not miss that ultimate felicity. Instead, they would endure in a state of what the Church called 'natural happiness' until the final redemption of the Last Day. Taken from the Latin *limbus,* meaning 'border', the word *limbo* has been widely used to suggest a state of being suspended inconclusively betwixt-and-between two options, though it might be more accurate to suggest that the concept of limbo by-passes the heaven–hell dichotomy altogether. There were, in fact two limbos, scholars argued. The first was a *limbo patrum* ('limbo of the fathers') for those who had died before Christ had come to redeem mankind. It was actually the *limbo patrum* to which the dead Christ journeyed (in epic-style *katabasis*) after his crucifixion and burial, setting free the souls in what was generally known as the 'Harrowing of Hell'.

Though mentioned in the Apostle's Creed, this idea has largely been lost from the modern religious tradition: the fate of unbaptized infants in our own age has seemed of much more moment. They were sent to the second limbo, the *limbo infantium* for those who had died unbaptized in infancy. This limbo has become increasingly controversial. In recent decades, Catholics have asked why there should be any discrimination at all, however slight, against sinless children who

Left: Jesus releases the righteous souls in his 'Harrowing of Hell', as represented in the altarpiece of the Church of the Holy Sepulchre.

79

Above: Lost in Limbo, apparently for eternity, the virtuous dead reach out in joy as the crucified Christ descends to the underworld to set them free.

had the misfortune of dying soon after birth. By 1984, Cardinal Joseph Ratzinger – later Pope Benedict XVI – was expressing the opinion that limbo had never been a definitive part of Catholic doctrine. It was, he said, no more than a 'theological hypothesis'. In 2006, a Church commission recommended the abolition of the entire concept in favour of a doctrine that those who died unbaptized in early infancy would naturally gain salvation. In April 2007 the recommendation was approved and the Vatican abolished limbo.

THE 'GOLDEN AGE OF HELL'

Alice K. Turner has identified a 'golden age of Hell', in the twelfth century, but the whole period of the Middle Ages was rich in writings on this theme. As we saw with Augustine, some of the greatest minds of the time applied themselves to the task of teasing out the most arcane details of damnation. 'What seems astonishing now,' says Turner:

> is the literal bent theologians brought to matters that do not lend themselves to the literal. Intelligent, educated men, who, if they had been born centuries later, might have explained the ineffable or metaphorical in terms of quarks and black holes in space, instead turned their attention to such considerations as whether food consumed during a lifetime would be part of the body at the resurrection.

But again, the concrete image seems far to outweigh the abstract thought, and it was in the visual arts that this infernal obsession found its fullest expression. Sculptors and wood-carvers worked grotesque demons and damnation scenes into choir-screens, pew-ends, the capitals of pillars and door-surrounds. For a few heady centuries, the diabolical became decorative. Everywhere the churchgoer looked, there were reminders of the fate awaiting those who chose the pleasures of the earth over the joys of the afterlife. But it was perhaps in the paintings of the era that we see hell's torments captured with most enthusiasm. Many great murals must have been lost, but enough smaller-scale works remain to bear testimony to an explosion of creativity. The thought of eternal suffering seems in some strange way to have unlocked the medieval imagination. Artists vied with one another to create the most outlandish hells, the most hideous monsters and the most pathetic inmates.

Naked now, their earthly trappings stripped away, lost souls hurtle downwards into the abyss, or bob about helplessly afloat in a fiery stew.

Left: A topographical feature for Virgil; a monstrous maw for medieval artists – here we see the Mouth of Hell through the eyes of an engraver of 1866.

Cheerful-looking devils sit around, snacking nonchalantly on the limbs of the sinful; others are at work, shovelling souls into enormous cauldrons. In many pictures, hell itself is given form as a demonic monster, its jaws agape, a devouring maw for those whose earthly appetites have damned them. The image of 'hell's mouth' appears to be another example of how the figurative became literal: it seems to have originated in a throwaway reference by Virgil (Georgics, IV) to the 'jaws of Taenarus'. This was really just a poetic description of the rocky gap through which the valley of Avernus led to the underworld, though it clearly hinted at something stronger and more predatory. The hint was taken with a vengeance by the artists of the Middle Ages, who created vast, spreading mouths, surrounded with fangs and stuffed with sinners. (Wooden hell-mouths were constructed as the infernal centrepieces for the hugely popular dramas of death and judgment in which the cycles of 'mystery plays,' staged by city workman's guilds, had their climax.) In some representations, the hell-mouth doubled as the genitals of Satan, once more underlining the link between earthly desire and eternal perdition.

These crowded canvases suggest the sheer number of the damned and the promiscuity of the lives they lived before. But they can't help also communicating energy and life; there is often an exuberant wit and a macabre humour about them. The carnivalesque quality of the medieval hell has frequently been noted – there is something almost festive about these works. This paradoxical sense of a view that makes death and damnation seem somehow life-affirming has also been evident in later reactions to the *Divine Comedy* of Dante Alighieri. One of the classic works of Western literature, this great poem attempts nothing less than a schematization of the afterlife, a comprehensive account of 'the state of souls after death'.

In its three books – each an epic in itself – Dante dealt separately not just with the Inferno but with Purgatorio and Paradiso, though he hardly need have bothered with the second and third volumes as far as many later readers have been concerned. This is sad, and unjustified from a literary perspective (posterity has in many ways 'missed out'), but is not really so surprising if truth be told. For the Romantics of the nineteenth century in particular, the poet's portraits of both Purgatorio and Paradiso pale into insignificance beside his nightmarish portrait of the Inferno. Few writers of fantasy have ever come close to him for sheer extravagance of vision, and none has even begun to rival the heartrending tales of human vulnerability we find here. Conducted through hell's chambers by the soul of the Roman poet Virgil, Dante meets up with old friends and acquaintances from fourteenth-century Florentine life. Brunetto Latini, a fellow-poet and Dante's own beloved tutor, but a homosexual who loved young men too much, has here to pay the price of his forbidden longings. Francesca da Rimini and Paolo, her brother-in-law and, eventually, lover, are condemned for their adultery to be blown endlessly this way and that by violent winds as once they were by the storms of lust.

Many of the damned are – their fatal sins apart – sympathetic characters, and Dante has to struggle hard to see how this hell could have been founded in the love of God. But his faith never really falters: in this respect, he is very much a man of his time, and though he can weep for the sinner he gives thanks for the overall scheme. In this regard, he would have found it hard to understand the

Many of the damned are – their fatal sins apart – sympathetic characters, and Dante has to struggle hard to see how this hell could have been founded in the love of God.

Left: The poet Dante is conducted on his epic tour of the Inferno. His *Divine Comedy* (1308–21) maps out the medieval cosmos in the most unforgettable of terms.

way in which his *Inferno* later came to shoulder aside its companion cantiche –
for Hell's sufferings can make no real sense when abstracted from the universal
order. And order is of the essence here: Dante gave his afterlife an elaborate
organizing architecture in which every vice and virtue, and every human being,
had their place.

The Inferno, as might be expected, is a vast and all-engulfing pit whose
precincts are entered through a great gate, above which is the famous inscription:
Lasciate ogni speranza, voi ch'intrate ('abandon every hope, you who enter').
But whereas most medieval hells are, as we have seen, anarchic in their crowded
chaos, Dante's is anything but – what can only be described as a 'beautiful' order
reigns down here. His journey through hell is to take him down into the very
bowels of the earth, through nine concentric circles, in which the different
sorts of sinners are grouped, descending through gradually deepening levels
of heinousness.

The first circle is not what we would understand as hell at all but the *Limbo
Patrum*. Dante sees several figures from the Old Testament of the Bible here,

Below: Satan, incongruously crowned, is the unlucky 'king' in Dante's underworld: he lies frozen in the very depths of the Inferno.

along with such luminaries of the pre-Christian past as Homer, Horace and Julius Caesar. Their only punishment is the sadness they feel at having been denied the gift of salvation, their homesickness for the heaven they will never know. In the second circle are the lustful – the great lovers of myth and history. Dante faints in his compassion for Francesca and Paolo. Next come the gluttons, and after them those who were greedy for wealth and riches. In the fifth circle are the wrathful and the slothful. Farther down in the sixth circle – since they sought to corrupt the minds of others with their sins – are the heretics who tried to pervert the teachings of the Church.

The seventh circle is given over to the violent, including those who did violence against themselves (the suicides) and those who did violence against God, by committing the sin of blasphemy. Deviousness and dishonesty are deemed worse than the more frank, straightforward sins, so frauds and flatterers have been consigned to the eighth circle. Seducers and sorcerers both have their separate niches down here as deceivers of different sorts; so too do hypocrites and those who have slyly stirred up discord. At the very centre of the earth lies the ninth, and deepest, circle, 'home' to Satan and to other traitors against their lords. Here is Judas Iscariot, the betrayer of Jesus Christ, his head eternally in Satan's mouth, whilst his nether parts are endlessly flayed by the devil's claws. Also here, however, are political traitors like Brutus and Cassius, the conspirators who assassinated Julius Caesar. Readers in the Anglo-Saxon world, familiar with Caesar's story through the play of Shakespeare, are accustomed to the idea of Caesar as a would-be tyrant, brought down in the nick of time by a group of idealistic republicans. In Dante's day, however, the assassins were seen as having rebelled against their ruler, a crime capable of upsetting the entire state.

In Dante's hell, Satan is shown in his essential nature: not strong and powerful but utterly defeated. It is over his helpless body that Virgil and Dante clamber back to ground level. They are then ready to start climbing the mountain that, in Dante's scheme, stands for purgatory, and the moral ascent required before the soul can win salvation. Around its slopes are terraces, this time assigned to each of the seven deadly sins: pride, envy, wrath, sloth, avarice, gluttony and lust. The punishments fit the crime – so, gluttony goes hungry, lust burns and sloth must expiate its idleness by endless running. Other penalties are less obvious: the avaricious must lay face-down on the ground to signal their grubby greed and their earthbound ambitions; the wrathful wander through thick smoke in token of the anger that once clouded their judgment. As the soul completes its punishment at each level, it is free to ascend to the next, spending a longer or shorter time there according to its earthly conduct.

At the summit of the mountain is the Garden of Eden, where the soul may go once its state of primal innocence has been restored. Here Dante has to leave Virgil, his guide till now – he must return to hell's first circle as a 'virtuous Heathen'. Another spirit will conduct him through heaven's nine spheres. This is Beatrice, beautiful and chaste, the great love of Dante's real life and the subject of his memoir of idealized ardour, *La Vita Nuova* ('The New Life', c.1293).

Heaven too has its hierarchy: the spheres of the different planets reflect the way the physical universe was thought to be constructed in the Ptolemaic model. First comes the sphere of the moon: because of the moon's phases, this was associated with changeableness. Here we find those who lived well, but forsook

In Dante's hell, Satan is shown in his essential nature: not strong and powerful but utterly defeated.

religious vows – leaving religious orders, for example. In the second sphere, that of Mercury, are those who lived well out of the desire for fame, while the third sphere – Venus – has those who acted out of love. The fifth sphere belongs to Mars, and is home now to those blessed souls who fought God's cause; the sixth, of Jupiter, has the heroes of divine justice. Saturn was associated with contemplation in the Ptolemaic scheme, so in the seventh sphere Dante meets the prayerful: monks and hermits. In the eighth sphere, amongst the stars, he encounters Saints Peter, John the Apostle and John the Evangelist, whilst in the ninth he finds himself among the angels. And then, at last, he comes face to face with God, in all his transcendent glory and his ineffable mystery. This, of course, he has no way of recording in earthly verse.

'IN THE MIDST OF LIFE…'

Thus summarized, Dante's *Divine Comedy* inevitably sounds schematic. The reality, though, is that it is one of the most moving stories ever told. At every stage, Dante has a chance to talk to the dead, to hear them describe their lives, to commiserate in their sufferings and to rejoice in their salvation. In the process, his poem considers every aspect of human life from love to politics, and makes an astonishingly ambitious bid to map out the medieval cosmos. Central to that universe is a logically ordered afterlife – the consequence and completion of our existence here on earth. Dante's work is a classic, a creation for all ages, yet it is very much a product of its time. Every civilization has had its epic, in which its most precious values are enshrined, but in most cases these hark back to heroic origins. The great poet of the Middle Ages had his gaze firmly fixed on the hereafter, on a life that seemed as real as – and far more momentous than – this mortal one.

This is hardly surprising. Though death comes for us all, whatever our place or time, it seemed to loom especially large in the medieval period. War was endemic, food frequently in short supply and medicine haphazard, to put it mildly. All in all, life felt fragile and death was never far away. This sense was only to grow in the decades after Dante's work was written (between 1308 and 1321). In 1315, the countries of northern Europe, from Russia in the east to Ireland in the west, were afflicted by what was to be a series of large-scale crop failures. The 'Great Famine' that followed would go on for five years and claim millions of lives. Stories of cannibalism circulated – some very likely true. But starvation was just the start: the famine caused widespread economic and social disruption, and in many places, law and order broke down completely.

Though the famine was officially over by 1322, the repercussions went on for several decades. Europe had barely recovered when, in 1347, the first cases of plague were reported. The Black Death, or 'Great Mortality', was part of a global pandemic that had already wrought havoc in more easterly regions of Eurasia. Caused by *Yersinia pestis,* a bacterium carried by the rat-flea, the plague caused terrible swellings, or buboes, in the armpits and the groin. Its spread was inexorable but often slow, so populations spent months in suspense, awaiting its arrival – perhaps daring to hope that they might be spared (some cities escaped completely). Between a third and half of the population of Europe died – in many areas even more – and for those who survived the sickness, there was the difficulty of coping in a society whose fabric was falling apart. The plague

subsided during the 1350s, but renewed outbreaks were by no means infrequent: for several generations, people lived with the feeling that death could come for them at any moment.

Hence the aesthetic of the macabre, the dominant force in west European culture throughout the late-fourteenth and fifteenth centuries. Grinning skulls were ubiquitous, delivering their warning *memento mori* ('remember, you will die'). Lines of skeletons cavorted together in the 'Dance of Death'. Often, seen in close-up, the dancers could be seen to wear the badges of different social rank, from royalty to serfdom, showing that Death (who was much personified) united all degrees. The display of these trappings also made the point that earthly aspirations were so much vanity. Whoever we were, we were dancing toward the grave.

Above: Death may always be with us, but in medieval times it seemed a constant companion: this picture shows plague-hit Florence in the fourteenth century.

A HALFWAY HOUSE

For its first readers, the *Divine Comedy* must have offered a strange combination of the familiar and the extraordinary. In one respect in particular its vision was different, even dissonant. If its Hell was recognizably rooted in the pit of the past and its Heaven chimed harmoniously with the Ptolemaic notion of the spheres, its Purgatory was more surprising in its conception. Dante's mountain may have meshed nicely with a scheme that saw the universe in terms of a single vast and vertically organized moral hierarchy, but Purgatory was more widely understood in terms not of space but time.

Dante could allow himself this latitude because, whilst not exactly new, the concept of Purgatory had yet to become fixed in the medieval mind. The feeling had been growing since very early in the Church's history that the division between Heaven and Hell represented too stark a dichotomy. There must, many theologians reasoned, be some intermediate state for those whose lives had been generally virtuous but less than perfect. By the fifth century, the idea had taken hold of a temporary, purifying fire – its punishments the same as those of Hell, but finite. Once the soul had received its chastisement; once its staining and corruption had been burned away; it would be fit to be received into Heaven for all eternity.

It was Gregory I 'the Great', the Pope from about 540 to 604, who first suggested that prayer or good works in this life might ease the soul's sufferings in the next. In the centuries that followed, this idea was developed and refined until an elaborate system of 'suffrages' emerged. These allowed the faithful both to make provision for their own eternity and to help speed their dead relations through the fires of Purgatory to Heaven. The system, as historian Paul Binski in *Medieval Death: Ritual and Representation* has remarked, 'came to be based upon an impressively simple, entirely calculable, rationale: that of the remission of a prison sentence.' Every soul that went to Purgatory faced either a shorter or a longer term of chastisement there, according to the relative imperfection of its mortal life. The completion of certain prayer regimes and the saying of masses on one's behalf (obtained by making an offering, payable to the priest) secured 'indulgences' – reductions in the amount of time to be spent by the soul in torment. In very special circumstances, a 'plenary' (full) indulgence might be granted: if the soul died at that moment, it would be allowed to proceed to Heaven without delay.

Protestants may regard this as the most outrageous sort of 'second-guessing' of God's judgment – for that matter, many modern Catholics look askance at such goings on. At the time, though, the system seemed a logical enough application of the rights and privileges that Christ himself had invested in St Peter, the first pope. 'And I say to thee: That thou art Peter' (Matthew, XVI, 18). Jesus continued (verses 18–19), punning on the Latin *petrus,* 'stone':

> And upon this rock I will build my church. And the gates of hell shall not prevail against it.
>
> And I will give to thee the keys of the kingdom of heaven. And whatsoever thou shalt bind upon earth, it shall be bound in heaven: and whatsoever thou shalt loose on earth, it shall be loosed also in heaven.

Left: Christ, from above the altar, explains His thinking to Pope Gregory I. 'Gregory the Great' was radically to reform Christian attitudes to death and judgment.

It was Gregory I 'the Great', the Pope from about 540 to 604, who first suggested that prayer or good works in this life might ease the soul's sufferings in the next.

The introduction of the indulgence system was at least to begin with a positive
step, dispelling depression and fatalism, and helping to re-energize the faithful.
Though many strove to live the virtuous life, few could feel that they were going
to die in a fit state to be admitted to heaven. Now, though, they could see a
chance of escaping Hell.

Binski has called this system the 'bookkeeping of salvation', and the financial
image is all too unedifyingly apt. The Church was – inevitably – a worldly as
well as a spiritual institution, and these two aspects were not easily to be kept
apart. The right to grant these 'indulgences' was a temptation for the Church, not
least in the way that it allowed the papacy to flaunt its spiritual power. In 1300,
for example, Pope Boniface VIII announced a jubilee year, declaring that all who
made the pilgrimage to Rome and confessed their sins that year would receive a
plenary indulgence. Two million people are believed to have heeded his call.
However, the payment of what amounted to a fee to have masses said for the
sanctification of the soul introduced a grubby note to what was supposed to be a
spiritual transaction. As early as 1245, Pope Innocent IV had let it be known that
those who contributed funds to the building of London's Westminster Abbey by
Henry III could expect an indulgence of 20 days from the pains of Purgatory. A
laudable project, no doubt, but a clear financial exchange for all that – and, by
the fourteenth century, indulgences were frankly being bought and sold. In 1344,

for example, Pope Clement VI issued no fewer than 200 plenary indulgences in England alone, to men whose pious offices had taken the form of generous payments to the papacy.

The sale of indulgences notoriously stirred opposition to the Church in late-medieval times and helped bring about the first rumblings of Reformation. Protestantism swept away the whole system, corrupt as it was: the final destination of the soul was up to God, it said. In Martin Luther's view, 'We should pray for ourselves and for all other people, even for our enemies, but not for the souls of the dead.' John Calvin dismissed purgatory as a 'fiction'.

Left: Philip II's palace-cum-mausoleum, the Escorial placed death and its various rituals at the very heart of religious and political life in Catholic Spain.

Right: Five centuries'
worth of royal bones lie
in the 'Royal Pantheon',
at the Escorial, in some
respects a modern,
Catholic version of the
Persians' imperial tombs.

DWELLING WITH DEATH

The Church's response to the religious rebellion convulsing Western Europe in
the sixteenth century was to fight fire with fire, launching its own 'Counter-
Reformation'. Far from abandoning its controversial doctrines, it insisted upon
them more firmly, even passionately – indeed, a new emotionalism was injected
into spiritual and ritual life. It was against this background that King Philip II of
Spain built the Royal Monastery of San Lorenzo de El Escorial in the mountains
outside Madrid, as a combined palace, monastery, university and royal tomb.

Building began in 1563, to a design by Juan Bautista de Toledo and Juan de
Herrera – massive, magnificent and yet strikingly severe. Completed in 1584,
the complex has a gridlike plan, in honour of its dedicatee, St Lawrence,
traditionally martyred by being burned on a gridiron. In a special Royal
Pantheon, along with the sacred relics of innumerable saints, were the remains
of Philip's predecessors on the throne of Spain. He too would be interred here in
his turn, as would many of his successors over the centuries. The monks of the
monastery attached to the palace prayed without ceasing for the repose of the
souls of Spain's dead kings, and endless masses were said to smooth their
passage through purgatory. If medieval times had seen an over-ingenious
'bookkeeping of salvation', here souls were being saved on an industrial scale.

Once the Escorial was ready Philip removed here, and from that point the
complex became his home. He had, more or less avowedly, chosen his dead
ancestors over his living court for company. His palace was effectively his tomb,
and he was to die there in a bare cell, just a stone's throw from his final resting
place in the Pantheon. That made a certain sense: the Escorial was the fortress
from which he hoped to lead the fight-back against the Reformation, and he saw
the souls of the dead as his allies in that war.

Today, the Escorial is generally regarded as Philip's folly, a monument to
morbidity and gloom, but there may be other ways of 'reading' his life and his
greatest building project. Between the 'black legend' of Anglo-Saxon
historiographical tradition, which waged a propaganda war against Spain for
centuries, and modern disapproval of the country's colonial project in the New
World, it is difficult to regard Philip's reign in a sympathetic light. Add in the
theories of twentieth-century psychoanalysis and the pathological view becomes
irresistible – but alternative perspectives are at least worth entertaining.

Philip's apparent embracing of the idea of death, his sense of solidarity with
the departed, will always seem strange and alien to us – but it need not
necessarily be written off as grotesquely 'gloomy'. Recent accounts suggest that
Philip was actually quite upbeat in his manner, full of intellectual energy and
enthusiasm for life. What his monument may actually commemorate is the
continuing connection which, in the Catholic tradition, exists between the living
and the 'faithful departed'. A 'bond of charity', Thomas Aquinas called this
connection in the thirteenth century, though as we have seen it was all too often
a sordid commerce. But the institutional shortcomings of the Church do not
nullify the possibility of a living and ultimately affirmative relationship with the
dead, and while we may see the belief as absurd, we have no business dismissing
it as morbid. That it seems so to most of us now is in large part because
Protestantism – for better or for worse – broke the 'bond' and set us at a new
distance from the dead.

chapter 4

THE ANCESTORS AT HAND

Bishop Diego de Landa of Mexico's Maya wrote about the Maya language and people in his book *Relación de las Cosas de Yucatán* (c.1566):

These people had a great – even an excessive – fear of death. They showed this in all the observances they offered to their gods with no other end than to get them to grant them life and health. But once death did finally come, it was something to see the weeping and lamentation for the departed, and the deep sadness that there was among the bereaved. They wept for them in silence by day, and with such heartrending cries by night that it hurt to hear it. They continued in extraordinary sadness for many days. They fasted and abstained in honour of the dead – especially the husband or wife – and said (of the deceased) that the devil had taken them, because they blamed him whenever anything bad happened, especially death.

They laid out the dead, filling their mouths with ground maize, which is their food, and a drink which they called koyem, and along with these a few little stones which they used as coins, so that

Left: For the Toltecs, the remains of the dead seem to have been a source alike of horror and of reassurance, their guarantee of their ancestral inheritance.

they would not want for anything in the afterlife. They buried the body either inside or just behind their houses, throwing one of their little idols into the grave; and, if the deceased was a priest, a few of his books; or, if he was an enchanter, his stones of sorcery and other gear.

That a people so abjectly afraid of death should choose to keep their dead at such close quarters may seem surprising, but human attitudes to mortality have seldom been straightforward. Perverse or not, the Maya kept this custom up for many generations, living atop the remains of their ancestors in their own homes. The practice had long predated them, moreover, as evidence of similar burials has been found in excavations at Tula, the capital of the Toltecs, whose civilization reached its height towards AD 1000. This longevity notwithstanding, the custom clearly seemed as strange to the Maya themselves as it does to us in some ways: they typically left their homes empty for a time after such burials, says Landa, till they could overcome their fear. In the longer term, though, they must have found the continuing proximity of their ancestors a comfort, a constant reminder, perhaps, of who they were.

ABOUT THE HOUSE

The ancestors also reminded them of what they owned. 'By continually curating the bones of deceased family members within their own domestic space,' suggests archaeologist Susan D. Gillespie, 'surviving members of the household may have strengthened their rights to material property'. The Maya may have had houses in the same sense that we do – built habitations – but they also had 'houses' in the sense of corporate kinship groups. Something of the same is known to have applied to the ancient Greeks, for whom the *oikos* ('house' or 'household') was the basic building-block of society. So far so commonsensical, perhaps, but we know from the great tragedies of Aeschylus, Sophocles and Euripides that these houses transcended the limits of this life to include the ancestors, whose will had to be attended to and whose wrongs had to be avenged. The *oikos* exerted a tug of loyalty that the developing structures of the state, or *polis,* found hard to contend with, creating tensions at the very heart of Greek society.

Similar traditions prevailed in some of the earliest known societies in history: at Çatalhöyük, for example, in Asia Minor, modern Turkey. This large settlement, one of the first places on earth that might credibly be called a 'town', flourished between the eighth and the sixth millennia BC. Archaeologists believe that it had anything from 3000 to 8000 inhabitants at one time or another, all living cheek-by-jowl. Yet not quite living communally: hundreds of houses have been excavated, and each has its own integrity, its own clear definition. There are no streets or alleyways between them – people came and went through overhead trapdoors and walked across their neighbours' roofs – but at the same time they do not share partition walls. There are gaps between them, albeit often only a few centimetres wide. It seems likely, therefore, that the 'house' as a structure gave physical form to the 'house' in the wider sense. Elaborate wall-paintings on many walls testify to a rich (though as yet largely mysterious) symbolic life.

Here, as among the Maya, the dead of the family were interred in the earth floor: scores of skeletons have so far been found. Sometimes separate skulls are unearthed, their features refigured with clay or plaster, as though a revered ancestor has been kept alive beyond the grave. A division may be discerned between those buried at the 'dirty' end of the house, where the kitchen and general living quarters seem to have been located (usually near the southern wall), and those at the other side, which was ritually 'clean'. For the most part, only newborn babies and tiny infants seem to have been buried in the 'dirty' zone, perhaps because they were not regarded as being fully formed individuals.

Even as it sprawled horizontally, Çatalhöyük grew vertically, houses being periodically filled in with rubble and then built upon anew. We do not know precisely what triggered the decision to destroy one house and to start another, but one factor must have been the limited amount of space available beneath each floor for burial. Though there was a degree of flexibility (the construction of raised platforms within the house allowed several generations to be buried), there were obviously limits on how many, living and dead, could reasonably be accommodated. But the result was that, as time went on and one layer of

Below: The idea of accumulating archaeological levels was thrown into fast-forward in Çatalhhöyük, the living literally living atop the dead.

occupation succeeded another, the entire settlement rose steadily, the living buoyed up by the bodies of the dead. Çatalhöyük, says archaeologist Ian Hodder, 'could be described as a necropolis as much as a settlement' – yet we have no reason to think that its inhabitants found that fact off-putting.

THE SHAMAN'S FLIGHT

Many peoples believe that their ancestors are around them all the time, though dwelling in their own different realm. We are surrounded by spirits, such peoples say – those of animals, trees, rocks and rivers and those of our own departed relatives, who still keep a (mostly) kindly eye on our affairs. The priest or shaman communicates with this realm on our behalf, makes peace with the spirit of the animal before we hunt and kill it, and flatters our forebears and soothes away their bad moods. All religions were once like this, it is believed (the evidence of the earliest cave- and rock-art is persuasive enough, as far as it goes) and this sort of belief has persisted into our own century, albeit in cultures of the sort once dismissed as 'primitive'.

Shamanism, as such creeds are called, is classically associated with the hunting and nomadic pastoralist peoples of Siberia – the Tuvas, the Buryat, the Chukchi, the Sakha (or Yakut), for example. But it is to be found in many different forms in many different parts of the world. Quite what degree of connection really exists between these various shamanisms is debatable – some anthropologists refuse to employ the term 'shamanism' because they feel it fails to do justice to the diversity of the cultures concerned. It is easy enough to imagine shamanism being transported from Eurasia to the Americas when the first 'Native' Americans began their migration across the Beringia land bridge, around 10,000 BC. But shamanisms of one sort or another have also flourished in Africa and Oceania, and it is harder to see these as being related in the same way. It is also often impossible to distinguish shamanism from those religions conventionally called 'animism' (or, more loosely, 'nature worship'), which are founded in a belief that there are spirits in all things. In practice, those conventionally called 'animists' are just as concerned with their relationship with ancestral spirits as they are with those of nature.

Below: A shaman from Tyva, Central Asia, dances in a religious festival; in his frenzy he will finally take spiritual flight.

The label is still serviceable, however. Whatever the differences between these cultures, the similarities are striking. All place emphasis on the role of the shaman, priest or 'witch doctor' as mediating between the mortal and the spirit worlds. Often, two alternative realms exist: an upper and a lower world, our own earth constituting a third, 'middle' world. Contrary to what might be expected, the underworld is not inhabited by the dead but by nature spirits; the ancestors live above, in heaven with the gods. In many cultures, however, the distinction is less clear-cut, since people may well consider themselves to be the descendants of their tribal totem animals. Whereas most are marooned in this 'middle', mortal existence and will cross over to the realm of the spirits only in death, the shaman can move back and forth between these worlds. The shaman is therefore in a position to consult the ancestors about the future, or to seek their assistance in healing illnesses or solving problems. If the ancestors have been offended, the shaman can appease them; it is through the shaman that the ancestors can make their wishes known to the community.

The shaman does not simply flit from realm to realm at will, for special ceremonies are needed to ease the passage to the spirit realm. Though in detail these vary enormously from culture to culture around the world, clear

Above: The shamans of the Siberian Yakut provided a connection between the realms of living mortals and the ancestral dead.

continuities may be observed. Typically, excitement levels are raised by noisy, monotonous music and rhythmic drumming, often accompanied by dancing or swaying. The effect of the cacophony is to exclude everyday reality, to dispel all consciousness of the world beyond the ritual. Consciousness of self also evaporates; everyone present is caught up in the mesmerizing fervour, but the shaman for a time takes leave of his senses and is transported – literally, as far as those watching are concerned – to the other side.

The shaman's trance can be compared with the cinematic 'dissolve' that signifies our shift from one level of experience to another, in this case a journey from this world to the spirit realm. Believers, however, see it as a symbolic 'death', an anticipation of the journey to the realm of the dead and that final journey on which one day we all must go. Asked by anthropologist Richard Katz, why his Ju/'hoan or priest was said to 'die' in his trance, and whether he 'really'

Below: Bedecked in porcupine-quills, a shaman of the southern Africa's Ndebele people makes a divination from the setting sun.

died, one Kung San (as the 'Bushmen' of southern Africa's Kalahari Desert are more correctly called) replied: 'Yes, it is the death that kills us all…but healers may come alive again.'

Pyschoactive drugs are often used to help promote the state of euphoria required for the shaman to take flight. In Siberia, the favoured 'entheogen' is *Amanita muscaria,* the fly agaric mushroom. This species is instantly recognizable to anyone who ever read a book of children's fairytales, its bright red top picked out with little flecks of white. Shamans among North America's Navajo or the Kiowa of Oklahoma traditionally relied upon peyote, a mescal-containing cactus, which was the mainstay too of Mesoamerica's pre-Columbian shamans. In the Amazon, an infusion was (and still is, by some tribes) made from the leaves and stems of the ayahuasca vine, while in the Andes the San Pedro cactus was used. Less exotic drugs, however, may play their part in prompting the abandon on which shamanic ritual depends – anything from coca to tobacco and alcohol. In the end, the vehicle does not matter: what is important is the trip, which enables the shaman to take to the spirit realm.

Shamanism has fascinated 'New Age' thinkers in recent decades, though obviously Western enthusiasts approach these religions with their own set of spiritual priorities. It is natural enough, for instance, that those who feel oppressed by the institutional structures of organized religion should be attracted both by the spontaneity and energy of the shamanic rite and by the apparent anarchy of its organization. It is no surprise that, in an age of global warming and 'green' politics, people should respond to the shamanists' reverence for nature. It is also understandable that since the 1960s many have been attracted by the prospect of attaining spiritual insight through the use of mind-altering drugs. And who would not be intrigued to see the shaman's trance discussed in terms of 'sacred orgasm'? One key thing that traditional shamanisms have shared, however, has struck no answering chord in the Western breast, and that has been the ongoing relationship of the living with the dead. This too is hardly surprising. In today's advanced industrialized countries, old age is not revered for its wisdom but disdained for its frailty; it appears to be all we can do to keep in contact with our grandparents. So, outraged though we may be by the destruction of the earth, alienated as we are from our official culture, we feel no special yearning for contact with our ancestors.

In Australian aboriginal tradition, ancestors have always loomed large. Once some say, they walked the earth with their surviving kinsfolk, as large as life.

DEATH IN THE DREAMTIME

In Australian aboriginal tradition, ancestors have always loomed large. Once, some say, they walked the earth with their surviving kinsfolk, as large as life. A story told by the Worora, a people from the Kimberley Plateau in western Australia, tells how Widjingara became the first man to die in our modern sense. When an outsider from another tribe came to snatch away a woman from his community, Widjingara sought to stop him and was killed. His wife, the black-headed python, went into extravagant mourning, cutting off her hair and plastering her body with ashes – the very picture of the grieving widow. She ordered his obsequies and had him buried, with every attendant honour, then wept and wailed till everyone marvelled at her devotion. But death did not then have the finality that we have come to expect, and it was not long before Widjingara was fully recovered from his fatal wounds. One day, he strolled back into camp with a smile and a friendly greeting for all his old friends. Far from being pleased, his wife was furious. She had wrenched at everybody's heartstrings with all her displays of mourning – and now here he was, back to make her look a fool.

Widjingara was not unnaturally stung by this reaction: he turned on his heel and walked off again, whence he had come. He would not be back a second time – and, from that time forward, nor would anyone else. The living and the dead now inhabited separate spheres, which communicated only through the mediation of the shamanic priest. This situation, it is said, explains the custom of exposing the dead on platforms so that scavengers could come and take their flesh before the bare bones were buried in the earth. If the body were left intact, the dead soul might be tempted to resume possession and walk the earth anew – it was better to leave no room for misunderstanding. In the event, ironically, Widjingara did not leave the world altogether but helped to ensure finality of death by taking the form of the native cat (in fact, a small marsupial). This scavenger was notorious for browsing on the bodies of dead humans, thus preventing their return to their communities.

The story of Widjingara can be seen as representing what Western tradition would call a 'fall', the moment of selfishness that blighted an ideal original existence. Though there are obvious advantages in the segregation of the living and the dead, there is understandable nostalgia for the days when death was not yet irrevocable and the 'departed' did not actually have to depart at all. This would appear to be the inspiration for the richly carved and painted *pukamani* ('funeral') poles erected on the graves of the Tiwi, who inhabit Melville and Bathurst Islands, off Australia's northern coast. Sometimes recognizably human in shape, sometimes stylized beyond recognition, these are inscribed with elaborate imagery which, to aboriginal eyes, offers vital data on the deceased. These might include his totem animals and plants, the whereabouts of his home, the lands over which he hunted and so forth. Weeks of work may have gone into its creation, but once it has been placed, the pole is simply left: the intention is not to produce a lasting monument. Rather, it comprises a physical equivalent in the land of the living for the body buried beneath, and it is allowed to weather and decay at a natural rate.

The Yolngu of Arnhem Land have found a more philosophical solution to the problem of mortality. For them, every human being has two souls. 'One soul', writes Fiona Magowan, 'is peaceful and returns to the land of the deceased to be incorporated with the power of that place as well as the person's homeland'. This soul is known as the *birrimbirr*. 'The other, known as *mokuy*, is a mischievous spirit that requires guidance away from the world of the living to the Land of the Dead and to the homeland.'

Much tribal ritual among the Aborigines, and among many other indigenous peoples across Oceania, is about the interaction between the living and the dead.

ANCESTRAL ASSISTANCE

Much tribal ritual among the Aborigines, and among many other indigenous peoples across Oceania, is about the interaction between the living and the dead. Inherited costumes and traditional totems evoke the memory of the ancestors, from whom all spiritual strength is seen as being drawn. Skin-painted patterning helps to keep alive the imageries of antiquity, identifying the living with their late forebears. Often, indeed, the skin is painted with grey ash or clay to replicate

death's pallor. Some Australian Aborigines paint themselves as skeletons. The 'mudmen' of New Guinea's eastern highlands paint themselves from head to foot with white-grey clay, wear bamboo tubes on their fingers to make them look like bones, and don large masks that turn their faces into smirking skulls. Their war dance warns the enemy that they will not merely be taking on the tribe's living warriors, but the ancestral spirits who will be fighting by their sides.

The idea that the ancestors will come to the assistance of the living has some currency even in Western European culture. Most famously, perhaps, there is the British tradition that the legendary King Arthur sleeps with his knights in the

Above: A blank clay mask, a jagged grin and bony-looking fingers of bamboo give the 'mudman' of Papua New Guinea the look of a skeletal ancestor.

103

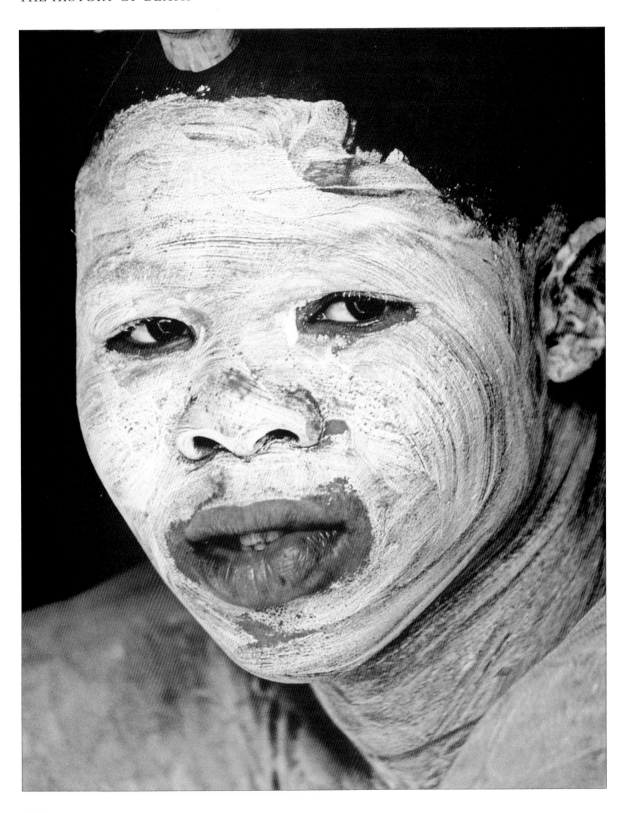

heart of a hill, but that they will awaken to save the nation in its hour of need. A variety of sites are proposed for their resting place, including the Berth, an Iron Age fort in Shropshire, England, and Craig y Ddinas, near Pontneddfechan in South Wales. Such stories are widely enjoyed, but generally dismissed as colourful 'folktales'; but there have been times in history when people have put far more reliance on ancestral aid. One of the most remarkable – and, at the same time, one of the most tragic – examples must surely be the episode of the Xhosa Cattle-Killing.

The story begins in 1856, when South Africa's Xhosa were feeling particularly beleaguered by the encroachments of the British on the one hand and by bad harvests on the other. But, just as they were beginning to think that they were doomed to conquest and enslavement and their culture to extinction, a young girl came forward with a message of salvation.

Nongqawuse was just 15 years old and, her parents having been killed in the wars against the British, she was being brought up by an uncle near the Gxarha River. On the banks of the river, she said, she had met the spirits of three of her ancestors, who had asked her to take on a sacred trust. She was to prevail upon her fellow Xhosa to slaughter all their livestock without exception, and to lay waste their fields and leave them to lie fallow. A fearful sacrifice, the ancestors acknowledged, but it would be rewarded a hundredfold when, on an appointed date in the future, a red sun would rise – not, as normally, in the east but in the west – and this strange new dawn would usher in a day of prodigies. The ancestors would return from the spirit realm and sweep the British before them in a mighty storm, returning the ancestral homelands to Xhosa rule. A new age of peace and plenty would begin – their herds would teem across the plain; their granaries overflow with golden grain. There was nothing vague about the prophecy: on 18 February 1857, the dead spirits would come streaming from a particular gap in a particular rock on the South African coast. But for these great things to happen, the living had to play their part, by destroying all their means of subsistence.

It says much about the Xhosa's desperation that they were ready to heed such reckless counsel, but in the weeks and months that followed they did what the ancestors had asked. Cattle were killed in their hundreds of thousands, heaped up in vast piles and incinerated; vast areas of growing crops were also burned. Hunger was already biting when 17 February 1857 came and the sun rose, just as usual, in the east. After this, it could be no real surprise when the ancestors failed to materialize: the Xhosa could look forward only to death by slow starvation. In the months that followed, their population plunged from around 100,000 to 30,000; by 1858, there were only 26,000 left. Far from having been saved, the Xhosa were left destitute and forced to enlist in the service of the British. As labourers for the colonists, they did become a marginalized group, just as they had feared, and saw their cultural inheritance all but extinguished.

Another beleaguered group who looked to their ancestors for deliverance from oppressors were the Lakota Sioux of the American West. They had been under pressure for decades when Jack Wilson or Wovoka, a shaman of the Northern Paiute in Nevada, had his vision for the renewal of humankind. On New Year's Day 1889, in the course of a solar eclipse, he foresaw the return of the Paiute ancestors and the removal of the Europeans. He himself appears to have

envisaged this liberation as following peacefully from a regime of moral regeneration and ritual observance, including a special 'Ghost Dance' in honour of the dead.

As the message spread among other native peoples, however, hotheads interpreted it as a call to arms. The idea took hold that the dance would summon up the spirits of the ancestors, who would lead the Indians to victory in war. Lakota braves grew particularly militant, becoming convinced that they must rise up in rebellion against the white man and that their consecrated 'ghost shirts' would shield them from all harm. How far an edgy US government contributed to the problem by overreaction is disputed by scholars, but restiveness had given way to violence by the end of 1890 and the authorities were openly panicking. The tension escalated through a series of skirmishes, culminating on 29 December with the massacre of 391 Lakota at Wounded Knee.

The Yoruba, of what is now Nigeria, had a bewildering array of *orisha,* or spirits, among whom, as in other shamanic traditions, the ancestors were key. It was vital to propitiate them, so sacrifices and prayers were offered constantly, and communication took place through the system they called *Ifa.* The priest took 16 small shells, called *buzios,* and threw them to the ground in a roughly circular pattern. From the way they lay, he could interpret the message of the dead. The beliefs of the Yoruba and other West African peoples found their way to the New World at the time of the Atlantic slave trade. There they would become the basis for syncretic creeds. The best known of these are Voodoo, as practised in Haiti, and Cuban Santería, both of which combine Catholicism with African traditions in which the ancestors are revered.

The office of *kpojito,* so crucial to the monarchical system of the West African state of Dahomey in the eighteenth century, was another way of involving the dead in the administration of the mortal world. When a new king ascended the throne, he took as his chief confidant and counsellor one of the wives that the late ruler had left behind. This *kpojito,* or 'reign-mate', ruled alongside him, pretty much on equal terms. Often, indeed, she was the real ruler of the kingdom. Scholars have pointed to this custom for the interesting insights it offers into the gender politics of the period, but it is arguably even more important to the history of death. The institution can be seen as offering a more-than-dynastic continuity, since the *kpojito* embodied the will of the dead king in the reign of his successor.

THE ULTIMATE ELDERS

In 1656, Spanish missionaries in the Peruvian town of San Pedro de Hacas, bent on rooting out pagan practices among the Indians, began searching a series of caves on surrounding hillsides. Over the next two years, they conducted a systematic 'census of the dead': one cave had 214 mummies; another 471; a cave at Ayllu Carampa housed no fewer than 738 mummified bodies. The relatives of these people treated them with much the same respect due to living elders, bringing them out at certain times of the year, offering them food and drink and even giving them new clothes. This was apparently in thanks for the good luck they had brought the community, especially at the crucial planting and harvest times. This was well over a century after the conquest of the Inca Empire, and the priests were shocked to see how persistent the old beliefs were proving.

Left: Lurid accounts of the Ghost Dance spread alarm among white settlers on America's Great Plains. In its original conception, the cult was one of peace.

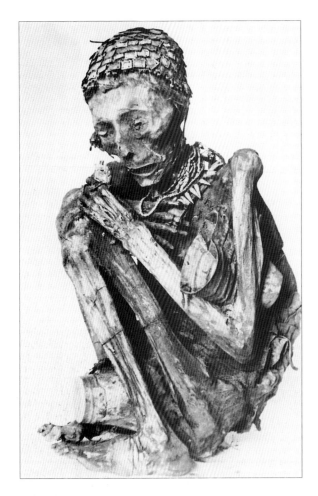

Above: Egypt apart, Peru is probably the home of the world's most celebrated mummies: the dry desert air having dried out bodies naturally.

When the first Conquistadors came to the Inca capital, Cuzco, in 1532, they were astonished at the status accorded to the dead. The Inca king looked to the mummies of his ancestors as his chief imperial advisers, and they were brought out to 'witness' all the ceremonies of state. They were treated with all deference and with every consideration for their comfort, as one amazed Conquistador, Pedro Pizarro, reported:

Most of the people served the dead...who they daily brought out to the main square, setting them down in a ring, each one according to his age, and there male and female attendants ate and drank. The attendants made fires for each of the dead in front of them...and... burned everything they had put before them, so that the dead should eat of everything that the living ate.

In the arid air of Peru, as in Egypt, bodies mummified naturally up to a point, but artificial means were used to perfect the process. These techniques had been employed for centuries before the Inca ascendancy in the Andean region: the first known mummies were made 8000 years ago by the Chinchorro, along the borders of present-day Peru and Chile. Though coastal fishermen, their settlements lay in the Atacama Desert, which is perhaps the driest environment on earth. Even so, they improved on nature, laying out the body before removing not just the internal organs but also the flesh, and then replacing the skin upon the skeleton. The face was fitted with a clay mask, and the head crowned with a wig of its own hair to create a fair approximation of the individual who had once lived. By 400 BC, peoples in Peru were placing their dead in a squatting position, with their knees drawn up beneath their chins, a practice that allowed the fluids of decomposition to drain away. Further refinements appear to have been introduced in Inca times, including a form of embalmment using a range of herbs, natural resins and a form of tar.

However it was done, there is no doubt that the results were impressive: 'Their bodies were so perfect that they lacked neither hair, eyebrows nor eyelashes,' the chronicler Garcilaso de la Vega would recall.

They were in clothes such as they had worn when alive... They were seated in the way Indian men and women usually sit, with their arms crossed over their chests, the right over the left, and their eyes cast down... I remember touching a finger of the hand of Wayna Qapaqh. It was hard and rigid, like that of a wooden statue. The bodies weighed so little that any Indian could carry them from house to house in his arms or on his shoulders. They carried them wrapped in white sheets through the streets and squares, the Indians falling to the ground and making reverences with groans and tears, and many Spaniards doffing their caps.

The Spanish burned all the mummies that they found, but did not succeed in stamping out the tradition entirely. Indeed, it can be argued that it endured into modern times. Soon, we find, the people of San Pedro de Hacas were managing without their mummies, giving the Catholic feasts of Saint Peter and Corpus Christi an emphasis all their own. The Spanish 'extirpation record' relates the testimony of one man, Hacas Poma:

And the other old men would pour out a little coca in the plaza and on the night of the festival day, they would perform the vecochina, which means that all the local kindreds and residential sectors would go forth, with the priests and ministers of idols in the lead, and the old ladies who accompanied them with small drums would beat them along all the streets, singing chants and dance-songs of remembrance in their language and their ancient style. They would recount the stories and ancient deeds of their mummies and their *huacas* [sacred sites] and...they would drink and get drunk. Until sunrise they continued in these exercises, engaging in contests and team matches between one residential sector and another, without sleeping the whole night through. According to this superstitious belief, the sector or team that fell asleep first, lost, and would suffer affronts about not knowing how to worship their idols right. The team that didn't sleep would carry off the victory and enjoy high regard, because this was the rite and the ceremony of their paganism.

If the dead could not be there as mummies, they could as memories.

A good excuse for a party? To be sure, and yet, at the same time this was obviously drunkenness with a purpose. Between the *chicha* (maize beer), the excitement and the exhaustion, the revellers would whip themselves into a state of something approaching delirium – and something not unlike the frenzy of the shamanic rite.

Even today, many in provincial Peru celebrate the festival of *Ayar Mayar Killa,* which literally means 'Moon when we carry the dead'. Held on the evening of

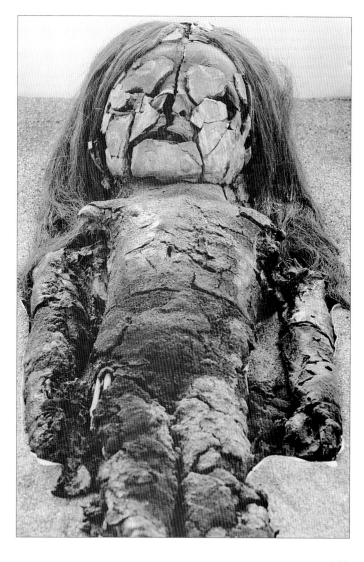

Below: Almost 8000 years ago, the Chinchorro of Chile's Atacama coast began making some of the world's earliest known mummies.

2 November, All Souls' Day in the calendar of the Church, this is a 'syncretic' festival in the sense that it is a grafting together of two traditions, the conjoining of a Christian feast with a pre-Columbian one. (That said, it should be remembered that the feasts of All Saints on 1 November and All Souls on 2 November themselves represented the syncretic 'bolting on' of Christian justification to pre-existing pagan feasts.) Food and drink in abundant quantities are taken to the city cemetery for a happy picnic while tending and restoring the graves. This is the day, writes Max Milligan, 'when graveyards come alive…'

> Stones are scrubbed and tombs repainted. Some bring portraits. All bring booze, and a merry inebriation settles over the afternoon. Huddles of heads in circles and lines nod and smile in recollection. Children scurry, shrieking with laughter, chasing each other round the graves of friends and relatives alive again in stories. Bones are dusted off, and placed somewhere safe. Loud mirth and quiet anguish surge and falter in turn. Cups are filled and spilled on the ground for Pacha Mama [the Inca earth goddess] and on to headstones for the dead to drink. The day draws on. The stories get longer and laughter louder. Silences open and close. As the light fails behind the peaks the raucousness recedes. Men stagger out to relieve themselves against the graveyard wall, while others snore through geraniums, arms wrapped round stone. A grandmother's skull adorned with a ribbon is cradled by a gently weeping man. He misses her and wants to take her home. It seems a good idea to everyone and he wipes his nose and smiles. Later, in the chilled darkness, drunks awake and leave with a flourish of goodbyes.

Similar festivities are held in Mexico, of course, for the *Día de los Muertos*, the Day of the Dead. Again, families flock to the cemeteries to tidy and tend their relations' graves, and to bring them presents of tequila and other drinks, favourite flowers and sweets, as well as special skull-shaped cakes of sugar. Often this is an opportunity to recall the tastes and preferences of the departed; dead children, for instance, will be treated with gifts of toys. At home, shrines may be prepared, with photos of the dead around the statue of the Virgin Mary, and with candles to symbolize the power of prayer. When night falls, the spirit of mischief rules as black-clad revellers roam the streets in *calacas,* or skull-masks. Traditionally, strings of shells were worn – the clacking din they made was intended to awaken the dead.

They would visit their family graves, weeping and wailing, and giving themselves over completely to their grief.

Mexico's *Día de los Muertos* falls in the autumn, in the 'dying of the year', just as it would have done in Europe, where the Christian feast of All Souls' took form. As Peru lies in the southern hemisphere, however, the *Ayar Mayar Killa* takes place in the spring, symbolically linking the ideas of death and fertility. *Radunitsa,* the ancient Slavic festival of the dead, was similar in important respects. This exclusively feminine festival was held in spring, when nature reawakened. It continued to be celebrated in parts of Russia at the end of the nineteenth century, despite the protests of the Orthodox priests, who were only too painfully conscious of its pagan origins. Every year, the women and girls of the village would take food and drink to the churchyard. They would visit their family graves, weeping and wailing, and giving themselves over completely to their grief. At a certain point, however, the mood would change, and mourning gave way to revelry as the dead were recalled in more irreverent, even scabrous

Far right: William Longespee's tomb in the majestic setting of Salisbury Cathedral affirmed his status – and that of his descendants.

terms. Again, drink would be poured on to the graves and food thrown onto the ground, allowing the dead to feel that they were sharing in the festivities.

Despite its theme, the *Día de los Muertos* could hardly be less dismal in mood. Death is not seen as something to dread but as something to be sent up in a spirit of fun. It is a time for mischief on the streets and rumbustious satire in the media. Something of the same applies to the corresponding British feast of Hallowe'en – a shortening of All Hallows' (Saints') Eve. Though the 'trick or treat' tradition of the United States, with its practical jokes and pumpkin jack-o'-lanterns, has been carried far and wide by American popular culture, it found a ready welcome in the British Isles, where it had in fact originated. Pre-Christian festivities for the dead persisted in the Celtic fringes (in Wales, Scotland, the Isle of Man and Ireland) which, being the poorer parts of the British Isles, sent a disproportionate number of emigrants to America in the eighteenth and nineteenth centuries.

If Hallowe'en could be said to have a single, original archetype, this is generally held to be the Irish festival of *Samhain,* when the dead were allowed to come back to revisit the living world. The aim of its celebrations was to welcome the good spirits and keep the evil ones at bay. Since the dead are privy to secrets that mortals are not, this was a good time to throw nuts or fruit and see how they

Right: Worshippers in Salisbury Cathedral would see, in the great tombs that surrounded them, reminders of the importance of the city's noble families.

112

landed or to watch the flight of crows as a way of divining the future – the name of the man or woman one would marry, for example.

Underlying all these upbeat festivals of death, of course, is a more general principle: that the more we make fun of death, the more we may disarm it and free ourselves of fear.

THE DYNASTIC DEAD

Built in the thirteenth century, Salisbury Cathedral represents a high point in the early English gothic – quite literally, with its 120m (400ft) spire. Inside, a narrow nave, graceful arches and slender windows place the emphasis on verticality: the whole massive structure seems suspended weightlessly. It is earthed, however, by massive medieval tombs, each one apparently more solid and imposing than the last. The earliest is that of William Longespee, Earl of Salisbury, who died in 1226 while the cathedral was still under construction. Like other aristocratic tombs of the time, it is basically a raised table topped by its occupant's full-length effigy. Longespee was Henry II's bastard son, but this impressive tomb undoubtedly appears to lend him a certain legitimacy.

In the south aisle, side by side and with their hands joined in prayer (though anything but ascetic in their sumptuously painted costumes), lie the effigies of Sir Richard Mompesson and his wife. They were powerful figures in Salisbury society in the fourteenth century. Still more stupendous, however, is the tomb of Edward Seymour, Earl of Hertford, with his wife Katherine, a riot of gilt and marble, its canopy rising extravagantly upward as though rhyming with the cathedral spire. Since Katherine was the sister of Lady Jane Grey, a Queen of England (if only for nine days), she was held to outrank her husband, so her effigy is shown raised slightly above his.

The detail is significant. Though they typically show their occupants in prayer, these great tombs are more about prestige than piety. For Western Europe's medieval aristocrats, the ancestors mattered as much as they could have done to any Siberian shamanist. It would be fair to say that their forebears were their fortune. An imposing tomb was an advertisement of dynastic power and pride, an assertion of the living family's inherited status.

Often this continuity was underlined by having subsequent generations buried together or in close proximity, as in Arundel Castle's Fitzalan Chapel, where all the Dukes of Norfolk have been buried.

Still more spectacular tombs were built with similar ends in mind by rulers in the Islamic world. That of Egypt's Sultan Hassan is awe-inspiring in its scale and beauty. Hassan was one of the Mamluks – slave-soldiers who seized power by military coup in the fourteenth century – so a cynic might say he was trying to fabricate some legitimacy for his reign. He certainly can have done himself no harm by building this vast mosque-and-madrassa complex. Four gigantic *iwans,* or porch-pavilions, are grouped in cruciform fashion round a central courtyard, in which a domed fountain played, evoking the atmosphere of heaven. (Unsurprisingly, given its origins among nomads from Arabia's deserts, Islam saw salvation in terms of arrival at a sort of stylized oasis, a lush garden where the weary traveller could rest, waited on by beautiful maidens.) Around this core were arrayed the halls of the *madrassas* (colleges of Islamic scholarship) and the mausoleum itself, beneath its towering cupola. In the event, Hassan was assassinated – the common fate of Mamluk rulers – in circumstances that remain unknown, so he was never to occupy the tomb over which he had taken such pains. Two of his sons are here, though, and his fame lives on in this monument, even if his body was never found.

The Mughal emperors of northern India also had a taste for tombs. The most wondrous of these is, of course, the Taj Mahal at Agra. This was built between 1630 and 1653 by the Emperor Shah Jahan for his beloved wife, Mumtaz Mahal, who had died in childbirth. Seen from a distance across its lovely gardens, shimmering in the heat-haze and mirrored in its long reflecting pool, it seems to be offering us a foretaste of paradise. Its central dome, round and bulbous, flanked on either side by minarets, it appears the picture of chaste simplicity. Up close, that impression gives way to one of astonishing exuberance, its marble walls exquisitely carved with a riot of ornamentation. In keeping with the broad-minded tolerance of the Mughal Empire at its height, these reveal not just traditional Islamic (Arabic) but Persian, Turkish and Hindu influences. The Taj Mahal is universally acknowledged as an illustrious monument to an undying love, yet it is also a monument to Mughal power and wealth.

PLACES OF PILGRIMAGE

The Mughal Empire was established in 1526; it seems to have been about a century before that when Hajji Ali, a Muslim mystic, died and was buried in Mumbai. Or rather, if his legend is to be believed, he died at sea a great many days sailing away, en route to Mecca for the great pilgrimage or Hajj. His coffin, it is said, was thrown into the waves, but miraculously floated home across the Arabian Sea. A great *darjah,* or shrine, was constructed at the spot where it eventually washed up, on some rocks that are cut off from the mainland at low tide. The mosque that houses the pilgrim's tomb itself became a place of pilgrimage, for Hindus as well as for the Muslim faithful.

Pilgrimages have for centuries been an aspect of religious life – and at certain times a social phenomenon of immense importance. A network of pilgrim routes ran the length and breadth of medieval Europe, for example, across which people travelled in the thousands every year. The shrines to which they journeyed

Left: Jerusalem's Church of the Holy Sepulchre was built to provide a fitting setting for the sacred spot for the tomb in which Christ Himself had been lain to rest.

Above: Up to five million Muslim dead may lie in Najaf's Wadi-us-Salaam cemetery – perhaps the biggest graveyard in the world.

were typically sacred tombs: from the Holy Sepulchre of Christ in Jerusalem to St Andrew's, Scotland. St James's tomb at Santiago de Compostela, in Galicia, Spain, vied for visitors with Thomas Becket's at Canterbury, England. There was indeed a degree of competition: the pilgrims had to eat and find accommodation, and profits were to be made by providing for them. An early form of tourist industry grew up to cater for their needs. The comparison is not flippant. While many pilgrims may have been spurred to travel by the spiritual motives, others sought a break from home and work, with abundant social (and maybe sexual) opportunities. Written late in the fourteenth century, Geoffrey Chaucer's *Canterbury Tales* describes a disparate crew of travellers, from a ploughman to a knight, from a miller to a prioress, from a merchant to a clerk, who come together to keep each other company on the road to St Thomas' shrine. The main point of the work is the collection of tales they tell one another in order to while away the time, but there is a great deal of comic conversational byplay in-between.

One thing that becomes quite clear is that however pious some of the pilgrims might have been, the pilgrimage played a vital part in the worldly life of the Middle Ages. The appeal of a shrine like Canterbury was a combination – to modern eyes uncomfortable – of the religious and the simply sensational. It had been consecrated after the murder of Archbishop Thomas Becket in 1170, by knights from the retinue of King Henry II. An old friend of Becket's, Henry had appointed him to his ecclesiastical post in hopes of having a reliable ally as head of England's Church, but had grown exasperated at his independent-mindedness. 'Will no one rid me of this turbulent priest?' he eventually cried out in his vexation, and his men took this as their cue. Becket was cut down in his own cathedral. His death outraged the entire Church, and he was canonized in a record three years, his tomb immediately becoming a site of pilgrimage. Within hours of his death, a blind woman claimed to have been healed simply by touching Thomas's bloodstained robe, and soon miracles were being reported at a rate of some 10 a day. Canterbury cashed in, entrepreneurially minded priests selling what purported to be vials of the martyr's blood and scraps of his clothing.

This aspect of medieval piety tends to strike us as weirdly 'fetishistic' today, but the sense of being in contact with the saintly was part of the point of pilgrimage. As tombs grew in size and showiness, open cavities or 'squeezing places' were sometimes left so that the faithful might feel they were getting closer to the sacred presence. Built after the saintly king's death in 1066, Edward the Confessor's tomb in Westminster Abbey was one example, though it was to be replaced when the Abbey was rebuilt in the thirteenth century. Another example, the tomb of St Osmund (died 1099), is still to be seen at Salisbury Cathedral.

To this day, Shi'ite pilgrims flock to the town of Najaf, on the Euphrates in Iraq, where Muhammad's cousin and son-in-law Ali is said to have been buried. (A rival tradition locates his resting place in the Afghan city of Mazari Sharif, itself an important destination for Shi'ite pilgrims.) Ali, who died in 661, is held in special reverence by Shia Islam as the Prophet's chosen successor: the first Imam or leader. Where Sunni Muslims look to the *sunna,* or tradition, of Islam as conducted through the line of Caliphs for their authority, Shi'ites seek theirs in the succession of Imams. The Imam Ali Mosque, in which Ali's tomb is

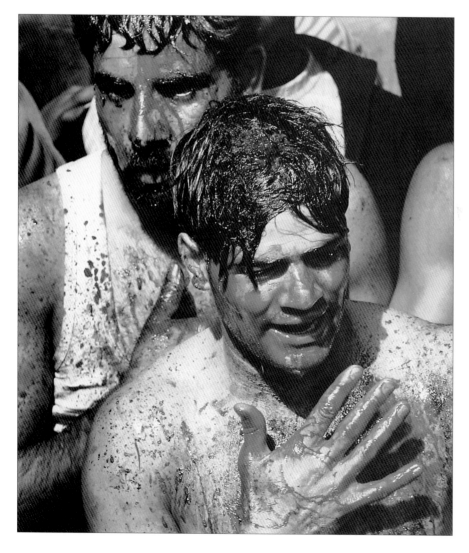

Left: Shi'ite pilgrims in New Delhi beat themselves in mortification for their sins in ritual mourning for Husayn ibn-Ali on the Day of Ashura.

117

contained, is a hugely important shrine. But if living pilgrims have made the journey here, many have chosen to journey here in death: beside the mosque is what may be the world's largest cemetery, the Wadi-us-Salaam ('Valley of Peace'), which extends across 6 square km (2.3 square miles). It is believed to contain more than five million graves.

Some 78km (48 miles) north of Najaf is the city of Karbala, the scene of a momentous battle in 680. Here Ali's son, Husayn ibn-Ali, the Third Imam, led a Shi'ite force against the army of the Umayyad Caliph, Yazid I, to uphold the true spirit of Islam as he saw it. But the Caliph carried the day, and Husayn was killed; his younger brother Abbas fell in the same battle. They were buried in twin shrines, which were soon among Shia's most sacred sites, and the core of what became the pilgrimage centre of Karbala. The mourning for these martyrs is renewed every year by Shi'ites on the Day of Ashura, when they beat their breasts – or, in some cases, even flagellate themselves – in ritualized grief. The secularist (though Sunni-leaning) Ba'ath government of Iraq did its best to discourage the annual Ashura commemorations at Karbala, though they were resumed after the fall of Saddam Hussein in 2003. Since that time, the shrines of Karbala and Najaf have found themselves in the front line in fighting between Shi'ite and Sunni groups, so the traditional pilgrimages have been badly disrupted.

As much a place of pilgrimage, in its way, is Lenin's Mausoleum, in Moscow's Red Square, built for the revolutionary leader on his death in 1924. Standing in the shadow of the Kremlin walls, its form is massive and squat. Built at first in wood (only seven years later was it reconstructed in stone), it was modelled in part on the tomb of Cyrus the Great of Persia. Lenin's embalmed body was placed inside in an open sarcophagus for public display, which was from the first the intention of the Soviet authorities. The exhibition of the leader's body was a logical continuation of the 'cult of personality' that had been created around Lenin in his lifetime. Over 100,000 Russians came to pay their respects in the first few weeks, and from that time on people queued daily for their chance to file past the body. On Stalin's death in 1953, he took his place beside Lenin in the mausoleum, but was removed again in 1961. Lenin was to prove a draw even after the fall of communism in 1989; supporters still come from all over the former Soviet Union to see his body. (Other communist leaders have been similarly displayed, from China's Chairman Mao to Ho Chi Minh in Vietnam. Juan Perón, the Argentinian dictator, was planning to exhibit his wife Evita in the same way before he was overthrown in 1955.)

Ironic as it may seem that an avowedly atheistic state should have set out to create a shrine of this sort, it is of a piece with the USSR's handling of death in general. As though attempting to synthesize a spirituality seen to be lacking in Soviet life, the authorities worked hard to establish a quasi-religious cult of remembrance around the millions lost during World War II – the 'Great Patriotic War'. Memorials were created in every urban centre, with all the paraphernalia of eternal flames, tombs of the unknown soldier and other monuments, and these were made a focus for civic ceremonies. In the same solemn spirit (though at the same time in an intriguing echo of the much more cheerful, old Slavic tradition), newly wed couples would go straight from the state registry to the local war memorial to acknowledge the sacrifice of the dead.

Left: Troops parade past the mausoleum of Ho Chi Minh in Hanoi – built in defiance of the late leader's express instructions.

119

Right: No community was left untouched by the fearful carnage of World War I. This memorial stands at Port Ellen, on the island of Islay, Scotland.

SPEAKING WITH THE DEAD

The losses of the Western allies in World War II were on nothing like the scale of the Soviet Union's. Germany's were grave, but there was little motivation for them to be memorialized. The reaction to World War I (1914–18) was, however, very different: the 'Great War' cut a swathe through British youth, including – indeed, especially – the privileged 'officer class' that might have been less vulnerable in earlier wars. When historian Jay Winter writes of 'communities in mourning', he is not exaggerating, and this was true not only in Britain and in Commonwealth countries like Australia, but in France and also in Germany. There were the usual support systems for the bereaved, but also a range of less familiar strategies, all with the common object of keeping the dead in mind. In particular, war memorials sprang up everywhere. In Britain, they are still to be seen, not just in every town and city but in tiny villages. Individual churches have their own memorials for congregants who were killed. So too do the country's most prestigious public schools, many of whose students were to go straight to the front and to their deaths, rather than to university. Workplaces also have memorials: Edinburgh's Waverley Station, for instance, has a tablet commemorating the railwaymen who fell; there is one for employees at the Upper Norwood Post Office in suburban London – and innumerable others, up and down the whole country.

But many families were not content to keep their loved ones alive just in their memories: spiritualism enjoyed a boom through the 1920s. The practice was not new. Attempts to communicate with the dead on the 'other side' had been going on since the mid-nineteenth century, and a series of 'mediums' had been unmasked as frauds. The secrets of the 'tilting table', which had astonished so many of the credulous at séances, had by then been rationally explained. Yet the belief was not banished entirely: that even the educated were prepared at least to flirt with the idea of communication with the dead is suggested by the vogue for ghost stories during the second half of the nineteenth century. Respectable mainstream writers, including avowed Christians like Charles Dickens and Elizabeth Gaskell, contributed to the genre. So too did such 'intellectual' authors as Henry James, along of course with specialized 'horror' writers like Sheridan Le Fanu.

The years following the Great War were to see a return of spiritualism to the centre-stage of social and cultural life. Reasoned scepticism was no match for the raw grief felt by so many. The author Arthur Conan Doyle is a case in point. The creator of Sherlock Holmes had already been lonely after the loss of his wife in 1906. Then, however, the war deprived him of his son, a brother, two brothers-in-law and two nephews in turn. This scale of loss was by no means unusual – and neither was his reaction, which was to hurl himself deeper and deeper into his spiritualist enquiries.

A man or woman with special powers to carry messages between the worlds of the living and the dead, the spiritualist medium is in many ways a modern, urban version of the shaman. That even the most educated should, in deep bereavement, respond to the spiritualist promise is not, perhaps, surprising. Even the strongest faith in the more conventional creeds does not provide for direct communication with those who 'went before' – and that, it seems, is a possibility which, at some level, we cannot help but crave.

chapter 5

THE DEMANDING DEAD

E ven today, on visiting a house in some of the remoter parts of rural Haiti it is the custom to pour water before the tombs of the dead, which are placed nearby. This is an offering to the ancestors of the household, whose goodwill it is always polite and prudent to secure before any meeting with the living members of the family. In different cultures, in different ways, the dead make claims upon the living, tugging at their loyalties, commanding their obedience from beyond the grave.

Mourning is not only an expression of grief, but part of the tribute we pay the dead. According to Plato, for an ancient Greek the culminating satisfaction of a long and honourable life was, 'having interred one's parents beautifully, to be beautifully interred by one's own children'. Their attentions were expected to carry on long after the funeral was over: women came regularly to the family graves, bringing offerings of cakes and wine. So seriously were such customs taken that those without children might well be moved to adopt an heir, just to be sure that these observances were continued. In several Latin American countries, as we have seen, gifts are still taken to the cemeteries

Left: The dead may make their claims on the living even in the most 'modern' society. Here a mourner visits a grave on Pawley Island, South Carolina, USA.

Women bring us into the world, and the implicit assumption seems to be that it is only 'natural' for them to take the lead in marking our exit from it.

each year on the 'Day of the Dead'. Many Chinese mourners, not content with interring their loved ones with toothbrushes and toiletries (so that they can keep themselves spruce in the afterlife), also burn paper models of consumer goods, including cars and TVs, to keep the dead happy. Even in the more self-consciously sophisticated societies of Europe and North America, people feel a duty to tend their loved ones' graves; Catholics pray each day for the 'Holy Souls' in purgatory. In some cultures, though, the dead have been a good deal more exacting.

A WOMAN'S PLACE

Mourning, like so much else, has tended to be governed by a double standard, a duty devolving more upon women than men. Women bring us into the world, and the implicit assumption seems to be that it is only 'natural' for them to take the lead in marking our exit from it. Thus the archetypal anguish of Our Lady at the foot of the cross, in Christian iconography, the grieving Greek choruses and the huddles of stage-Irishwomen 'keening'.

But women have sometimes been expected to do rather more than weep and wail and tear their hair. Visiting the Berawan of Borneo in the 1970s, Richard Huntington and Peter Metcalf found widows being 'cooped up for as many as eleven days in a tiny cell made of mats, next to the corpse.'

> She may not bathe, and may…eat only the poorest of foods, which she 'shares' with the deceased… She suffers because of the vengeful soul of the deceased. Its envy of the living, caused by its own miserable state, is softened by the spectacle of the hardship visited on those it formerly loved.

There have been cultures in which widows had it even harder. The Moroccan Muslim traveller Ibn Battuta was in for a shock when he witnessed a funeral in India in the 1330s. There, in a hollow by a lake, he saw a crowd assembled around a large, burning pyre; among mourners and musicians, some fifteen men stood around with bundles of kindling, and another ten with long poles. With the other mourners stood the dead man's widow: this was only to be expected, perhaps, but Ibn Battuta was staggered by what happened next. The woman 'joined her hands above her head in salutation to the fire and cast herself into it.' At the same moment the drums, trumpets and bugles were sounded, and men threw on her the firewood they were carrying and the others put those heavy balks on top of her to prevent her moving, cries were raised and there was a loud clamour. When I saw this I had all but fallen off my horse, if my companions had not quickly brought water to me and laved my face, after which I withdrew. (Ibn Battuta, III, p. 75)

The rite of *sati* was practised in parts of India for many centuries; the Sanskrit word means 'the woman who chooses the right path'. The widow who did so would be greatly honoured, and might even be worshipped as a goddess – though these rewards were, of course, necessarily posthumous. Although this was, in theory, a voluntary self-sacrifice, widows who failed in their duty could expect only to be ostracized, or to be placed on the pyre by force. The rite was regarded as the culminating moment of the marriage: the dead man and his widow would sometimes be dressed in their wedding clothes.

The origins of the custom are unclear. The presence of widows in a monogamous society might well have been seen as potentially destabilizing, but the old Brahmanic texts have nothing to say on the subject of *sati*. The practice is first recorded at the time of the Gupta Empire, in the fifth century AD, but was suppressed by some of India's Muslim Mughal rulers. It never died out completely, though, and in fact bounced back to have its heyday comparatively recently, from the final decades of the seventeenth century onwards.

Even then, the number of women involved were comparatively small, since *sati* was confined to the subcontinent's highest castes: at most, about 1 per cent of women would have ended their lives this way. Not that this diminished the tragedy for the many thousands who had to brave the flames down the decades. By the early nineteenth century, widows were being immolated with their husbands at a rate of around 600 times per year across the subcontinent as a whole, though the majority of cases were recorded in Bengal and other northern regions. The British were appalled at what they called 'suttee' and did their best to stamp it out, banning it altogether in 1829. It continued, however – lent impetus, it has been suggested, by laws allowing widows to inherit property.

WANTING BLOOD

In Benin, as the Portuguese called the West African kingdom whose own people referred to it as Edo, regular offerings were made to Ogiuwu, the 'King of the Dead'. He was said to 'own the blood' of all living things, which might be taken figuratively to mean that one day all must die, but was interpreted more literally at the *Ugie Ogiuwu*. An altar was set up outside the royal palace, and there the Oba – Edo's combined high-priest and king – ritually slew a man, a woman, a goat and a sheep in Ogiuwu's name. These were by no means the only human sacrifices on the festive calendar: another involved a dozen criminals being beheaded

Below: A goat is sacrificed at a religious ceremony in Benin, continuing the custom of centuries.

as an offering to the Oba's father. While the Oba called on the late ruler to protect his kingdom throughout the coming year, the blood of the victims was cast over the sculptures in the dead king's shrine.

The idea that the dead might in some sense be sustained by the blood of the living helps to explain the enduring symbolic power of the revenge tradition. That the dead might actually want to drink the blood of living mortals is the founding idea of the ancient Slavic myth of vampirism, given a new lease of life in the horror fiction and films of modern times. The 'undead', chill and pallid, are parasitical on the warmth and vigour of the living, which they can acquire for themselves only by sucking forth their blood. Something of the same can be seen in the sacrificial traditions of the Asante; in the seventeenth century, their kingdom lay to the west of Benin in what is now Ghana. Like many other cultures, they gave their departed kings two funerals: one after death, and another once their flesh had decomposed. It was at this point that they were placed with final pomp in the *Bantama,* the hall of the ancestors. Each year, in early October, the celebrations began, but while the king got drunk with his nobles, his executioners were roaming the streets of the city. Anyone incautious enough to cross their path was seized, but most lay low, and so the soldiers would seek out known enemies of the king wherever they were cowering and bring them back to the palace to be placed in chains.

Next day, the unfortunate victims were driven through the streets to the *Bantama,* where the skeletal remains of the ancient kings had been readied for a feast. Each in his own cubicle, the late monarchs were removed from their coffins, adorned with gold jewellery and laid out on beds; beside them were tables with vessels for food and drink. Each table had a chair, and beside each was propped a musket: a status symbol, and a mark of the power over life and death. The living ruler went round each in turn, listing the achievements of his reign in the most glowing terms and begging for his protection, offering him a drink and pouring a libation on to the earth before him. Then, to the sound of drumming – 'death's march' – a victim was hustled in, hurled to the floor and then beheaded. His blood, captured in a basin, would be smeared over the chair, the table, the eating and drinking vessels, the musket and even the skeleton itself – as symbolic nourishment – before the king moved on to the next cubicle and the ritual was repeated. The process had to go on until all the ancestors had been served; only then could their continuing goodwill be relied upon.

A less deadly form of blood-sacrifice – this one self-administered – is described by the early anthropologists Sir Baldwin Spencer and Francis James Gillen. At the end of the nineteenth century, they spent time among the Warramunga of central Australia, for whom the rites of mourning might start in advance of death itself:

> Some of the women, who had come from all directions, lay upon the body of the dying man; others stood or knelt all around it, pushing the points of their digging sticks into the tops of their heads, thereby causing wounds from which the blood ran down over their faces. They kept up a continuous wailing all the while.

A man, they report, is completely carried away in his grief. He 'rushes on to the scene', they say:

screaming with pain and brandishing a stone knife. As soon as he reaches the camp, he makes such deep incisions across his thighs, into the muscles, that, unable to hold himself up, he finally falls to the ground in the midst of a group; two or three of his female relatives pull him away and apply their lips to his gaping wounds while he lies senseless.

The self-laceration continues after the person dies, and is indeed renewed at intervals over the next two years, women reopening their original wounds with red-hot sticks.

Human sacrifices were also offered by the Asante when their mortal monarch died, but the rationale for this was rather different. From childhood, the king was attended by a group of boys of his own age, who were carefully selected for their grace and beauty. This was important, because these *akrafo* would grow up to sit before the king in his court, collectively a living, physical, externalized embodiment of his soul. Their good looks – and the distinctive golden pectorals they wore – underlined the handsomeness and generosity of the ruler's spirit. At their most mundane, they were his bodyguard: if need be, they were prepared to die for him, but it made sense that they should also die with him when his life came to an end.

Something of the same thinking may have been implicit in the sacrifices of human victims by other cultures, conducted as part of the obsequies for their

Left: An outsized figure plunges a victim into a pail in a scene from the Gundestrup Cauldron (first century BC), in what is apparently an act of human sacrifice.

Right: Seated victims wait helplessly, the executioners ready to dispatch them as attendants for a Natchez chieftain in the afterlife.

Temple.

dead rulers. Julius Caesar said of the Celtic Gauls that 'It is only a short time since the slaves and clients…loved by the dead man were cremated along with him when the funeral was properly carried out.'

The assertion has the ring of hearsay ('It is only a short time since…') but, while archaeologists are properly careful in their claims, a certain amount of what looks like supporting evidence has been found. The 'Gundestrup cauldron', for example, is a silver-plated bowl, or *krater,* consigned to the depths of a peat-bog some time in the first century BC, apparently deliberately. One of its details shows a human victim being drowned in a pail by a larger figure who may be a druid priest. At Hohmichele, Germany, in what otherwise resembles a 'wagon burial' of the sixth century BC, a couple have been buried together. Did they really die at the same time, and both by natural causes? It is not impossible, but seems unlikely. Further bodies were laid to rest with less ceremony within the same mound. Were these the lord's retainers, sacrificed when he died? Another apparent case of Celtic 'sati', this one dating from between 400 and 100 BC, was discovered in a mound at Hoppstadten, near Trier, Moselle: here what seems to be a whole family group was found. Another late-Iron Age cemetery, at Carrowjames in Ireland's County Mayo, has yielded a number of graves in which children have been buried – presumed sacrificed – with the adult dead.

'HE SUMMONS ME...'

Glorified 'grave goods'? When all was said and done, slaves were so much property. Their lord was considered to own them, body and soul. They may therefore have been sacrificed simply as items of great value. Or, of course, they may have been intended to act as servants for the afterlife. Then again, like the Asante *akrafo,* both slaves and family members may have been regarded as in some sense an aspect of the patriarch's personality, his selfhood, so that it seemed fitting that they left this life when he did. The Scandinavian-style ship-burial described by Ibn Fadlan (*see* Chapter 1) included the sacrifice of a slave-girl. Before she was murdered, we are told, she was three times lifted up above the pavilion containing her lord, each time being seen to murmur briefly before she was lowered. 'I quizzed the interpreter about her actions,' the Iranian traveller reports,

Below: Just a hapless criminal? Or, as many scholars insist, a noble killed in sacrifice? Beautifully preserved, 'Tollund Man' endures as an enigma.

And he said, 'The first time they lifted her, she said, "Behold, I see my father and my mother." The second time she said, "Behold, I see all of my dead kindred, seated." The third time she said, "Behold, I see my master, seated in Paradise. Paradise is beautiful and verdant. He is accompanied by his men and his male-slaves. He summons me, so bring me to him."'

The formula places the slave-girl's lord above her own parents and her kindred in her spiritual hierarchy, which makes explicit her role to serve as his handmaiden for eternity.

The Natchez of the Mississippi Valley were unique among North America's indigenous peoples in regarding their chief as the 'Great Sun', a kind of god. He was, they believed, a younger brother to the heavenly sun, the source of all light and life, and so his passing was a truly cataclysmic event. When he died, he was quietly laid out on a feather-fringed mat in his royal finery; his face was painted red, like that of the setting sun. Not until three days later did his mourning officially begin: a shout of desolation was raised by those around the chief, and taken up from village to village through the land of the Natchez.

The chief was then borne in procession to a tall earth pyramid, on top of which stood a temple. Outside the temple, his wives and servants and a sister and a brother all sat waiting. They had already taken a last meal: balls of tobacco compacted in water and containing enough toxins to leave them in a semi-

Below: Researchers pore over the remains of 'Lindow Man', unearthed in northern England – almost certainly a sacrificial victim.

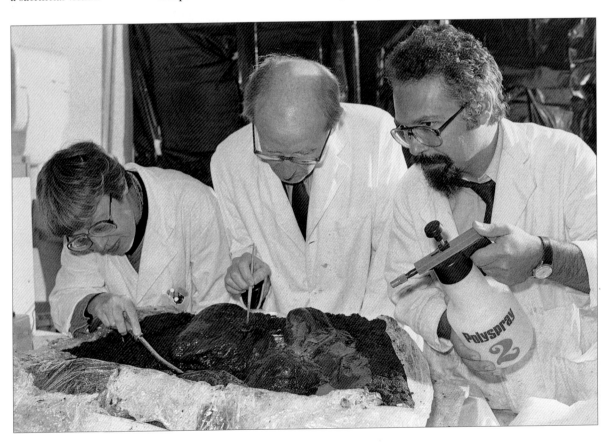

130

conscious stupor. It was thus the easiest thing in the world for an executioner to dispatch them with a garotte of plaited plant fibre, so that they could go with the Great Sun to his resting-place. The dead were buried in the earth for a time so that the flesh would rot, leaving only the 'bone soul'. The skeletons were then disinterred and placed in baskets in the temple. Only now, it was believed, was the Great Sun's soul at liberty to take flight for the highest heavens to be reunited with its heavenly brother.

Not all sacrificial victims were killed to keep their lords company in the afterlife. Some, like those found preserved in the bogs of Britain, Ireland and Jutland, were ritually killed but interred alone. They appear to have died to appease the gods of Germanic and Celtic tribes. 'Haraldskaer Woman' and the 'Tollund Man' were both discovered in Jutland, Denmark, their bodies preserved – effectively 'pickled' – by the still, acidic water of the peat bog. Though some archaeologists believe that the Tollund Man was no more than a criminal, executed and then dumped, others disagree, pointing to the fact that he appears to have eaten a special meal of bread just moments before he died. There are good grounds for believing that the Haraldskaer Woman had been a sacrificial victim: she appears to have been tortured before she died.

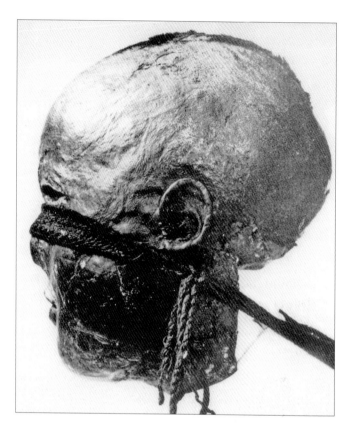

Above: 'Windeby Girl', barely a teenager, wore a blindfold of coloured cloth when she was deliberately drowned in a bog in Schleswig-Holstein.

When we come to the 'Lindow Man', discovered in 1984 at Lindow Moss not far from Manchester in northern England, the case is more compelling still. He had apparently had his skull fractured by repeated blows before having his throat cut. Finally – and surely superfluously – he had been garotted with a length of sinew. He too had eaten a special meal. There may have been some ritual reason for this threefold 'overkill'. His body was marked with the copper-based dye that was distinctive to the Celts and is conventionally known as 'woad', and he seems to have died in AD 100 or thereabouts. Study of his fingernails suggests that he was unaccustomed to manual work, indicating that he had been one of his society's more privileged members before his death. Another man found nearby seems to have died at much the same time, though the carbon-dating method has a margin of error of 150 years. And then there is the 'Windeby Girl', just turned a teenager when she was dispatched: she was preserved by the peat of another bog in Schleswig-Holstein.

Something in the region of 100 bodies have been found preserved in northern Europe's peat bogs, most dating from the Celtic era. We cannot know for sure how they all met their fate, but the evidence for some sort of sacrifice is overwhelming. How the victims were chosen, we do not know: a slave-owning society would have considered the lives of its slaves to be disposable, of course, but several of these victims seem to have come from a higher rank. This, however, would simply have increased their sacrificial worth, impressing the gods that those who offered them 'meant business' – if ingratiating themselves with deities was indeed the aim.

GIFTS FOR THE GODS

That was certainly what the Roman writer Lucan thought, describing 'those Gauls who propitiate with human sacrifices the merciless gods Teutas, Esus and Taranis – at whose altars the visitant shudders'. A Roman poet is not a modern scientific ethnologist, of course, and we have to be wary of such testimony, but the bog-bodies do lend his statement a degree of credence. So too, perhaps, do the horrific finds made at Byciskala Cave in the Czech Republic, where 40 bodies, mostly female, were discovered. All had been decapitated, and their hands and feet cut off besides. A skull, carved into a drinking cup, lay nearby; as did a pair of horses, cut into quarters. The evidence suggests that they were ritually killed some time in the sixth century BC, which makes it hard to dismiss Lucan's claims as Roman propaganda.

'It was their religion,' writes Tacitus concerning Britain's Celts, 'to drench their altars in the blood of prisoners and consult their gods by means of human entrails.' Again, the charge is not inherently incredible. Across the ancient world (in Rome as well), seers were accustomed to watch the twitchings of the innards of sacrificed animals to divine the future, much as the Yoruba priest 'read' the way his seashells fell when cast on the ground in the Ifa ceremony or, for that matter, as the Irish tried to tell their future from the fall of fruit or nuts or the flight of birds. Given that a human victim might be considered a more prestigious offering than an animal, it is not on the face of it impossible that such sacrifices should have been made. The Greek historian Diodorus Siculus, writing in the first century BC, described a slightly different form of divination:

> In matters of great concern they devote to death a human being and plunge a dagger into him...and when the stricken victim has fallen they read the future from the manner of his fall and from the twitching of his limbs, as well as from the gushing of his blood.

For what it is worth (and he may simply have read the same earlier source as Diodorus Siculus), Strabo corroborates this claim: 'They would strike a man who had been consecrated for sacrifice in the back with a sword, and make prophecies based on his death-spasms.' Caesar's troops, according to Lucan, went as far as felling one grove that had been sacred to the 'barbaric gods' and in which 'every tree was sprinkled with human blood'. 'Some tribes,' wrote Caesar: 'build enormous images with limbs of interwoven branches which they then fill with live men; the images are set alight and the men die in a sea of flame.' This charge too is confirmed by Strabo, who writes that:

> Having devised a colossus of straw and wood [the Celts] throw into it cattle and wild animals of every type and human beings, and then they make a burnt offering of the whole thing.

Needless to say, no archaeological evidence has been found to support the

Needless to say, no archaeological evidence has been found to support the 'wicker man' story, but for all that it is conceivably true.

'wicker man' story, but for all that it is conceivably true. If the gods of the Celts were indeed to be propitiated by acts of cruel slaughter, then it is easy to see how it might be a case of 'the more the better'.

HUNTING HEADS

That the gods might like sacrificial offerings makes sense; that the ancestors might crave blood has a certain symbolic logic; but is it possible that the living derive any benefit from human sacrifice? Another charge against the Celts that archaeology supports is the practice of headhunting. According to Diodorus Siculus:

> They cut off the heads of enemies slain in battle and attach them to the necks of their horses. The bloodstained spoils they hand over to their attendants and carry off as booty, while striking up a paean and singing a song of booty.

Below: The Macas, a Jivaro tribe from the forests of Ecuador, prepared this shrunken head as recently as 1963.

Above: The Iban of Borneo harvested heads as deliberately and determinedly as they cut their crops: the activities were ritually analogous, it seems.

It is clear that the Greco-Roman writer was repelled not just by what he considered to be the barbaric bloodthirstiness of this custom, but also by its lack of 'sporting' spirit or chivalry: 'It is bestial to continue one's hostility against a slain fellow man.'

All the indications are, however, that the Celtic warrior kept his prize, not out of 'hostility', but out of a fierce and joyful pride in his victory and, even more important, out of a sense that by doing so he somehow took possession of his enemy's strength and warlike prowess. It is clear from the recurrence of the severed-head motif in Celtic art that the head was regarded as the seat of the human soul. To make the heads of prestigious enemies one's own property was in some sense to store up spiritual capital, as well as boosting one's own image amongst one's earthly peers.

But headhunting is not necessarily all about taking trophies in a spirit of individualistic vainglory. Some cultures feel that there is only so much spirit, so much identity to go round. The Jivaro of the Ecuadorian rainforest traditionally believed that the dead were always stealing identities, seducing men and women away to join them, and that these identities had to be replaced. Unusually, then, Jivaro 'mourning' was not about remembrance of the dead. On the contrary, it was, in Anne Christine Taylor's word, a 'disremembering', a deliberate effort of forgetting. New identities would then be secured in tribal war. The heads of slain enemies were carefully skinned, boiled and dried, then stuffed and sewn before drying. The result was the notorious shrunken head, or *tsanta*. New Guinea's Marind-Anim saw the problem in terms of a dearth of available names: when they took a head from an enemy, they took his name for one of their children.

In other cultures, headhunting is regarded as a way of marking the age-old rhythm of death and rebirth. Working among the Iban of Borneo in the early 1950s, Derek Freeman found the idea of headhunting explicitly associated with the growing cycle. One chant directly compared the defeat of the Iban's enemies and the harvesting of their heads with the cutting of the rice on which the community relied for food. The idea of life and death as a ripening and reaping has had a place in the Western tradition since Classical times, but in some cultures the connection has seemed central. America's Mississippian civilization is a case in point. This culture came to prominence towards the end of the first millennium AD, and built a major urban centre at Cahokia, near modern-day St Louis. Whilst there is no evidence of Mississippian headhunting, pictures inscribed on artworks of copper or mica sheets do show what appear to be scenes of human sacrifice. In one, a priest smashes a victim's skull with a ceremonial mace in the form of a maize plant: human blood, it seems, was the life-giving rain that helped the corn crop grow. Among the Aztecs of Mexico, all children born on certain days were marked out for sacrifice: they would have their throats ceremonially slit to mark the festival of the rain god, Tlaloc. The symbolism of their sacrifice was as cruel as it was compelling: their cries and tears suggested the sound of storms and the fall of rain.

The vast majority of the Aztecs' ritual killings were, however, designed to secure the food supply not of humanity but of the gods. Such sacrifices were offered on a massive scale. At one single festival, it is claimed, well over 70,000 prisoners were ritually murdered over five days of non-stop slaughter. Such numbers seem quite literally incredible: simply handling so many prisoners would surely have been impracticable. There seems no doubt, though, that prisoners in their thousands were regularly slain. Aztec images show them standing in line, waiting patiently for death. The queue would take them to the top of a great pyramid, where they were lain upon a big stone altar, beside which stood the priest, his knife of obsidian (volcanic glass) raised in readiness to strike. With a single blow, he opened up the victim's chest, and with his other hand he seized the beating heart, which he held up high above his head to show the gods.

The most rapacious of the Aztec deities was Huitzilopochtli, god of the sun and war: he was believed to be insatiable in his hunger. Aztec tradition held that the earth had already lived through five stages of existence, the first four of which had ended in terrible destruction. The fifth catastrophe was impending –

The idea of life and death as a ripening and reaping has had a place in the Western tradition since Classical times, but in some cultures the connection has seemed central.

and the moment when it came depended entirely on Huitzilopochtli's whim. Hence the desperation with which they sought to win his favour. The longer life went on without the expected calamity coming, the firmer the belief that the policy of appeasement through mass-sacrifice was working. Bad news indeed for the countless thousands of young men among the Aztecs' neighbours, whose lives were to be expended in its name.

The Spanish sources from the time of the conquest are in agreement that the Aztecs practised ritual cannibalism – but they are also in agreement that, despite their impressive social organization, the Aztecs were fundamentally barbaric heathens. Modern scholarship has tended to explain (and thereby palliate) such practices in anthropological terms, rather than trying to examine the evidence that they actually took place.

There is no doubt, though, that cannibalism can be understood as something rather more than squalid savagery, and, if the Aztecs didn't do it, other peoples assuredly have. Ritual cannibalism appears even to have predated our humanity: there is evidence that it took place amongst our hominid ancestors, including *Australopithecus,* almost three million years ago. It is not something that *Homo sapiens* was to 'outgrow' through evolution, however. If we are reluctant to accept the anecdotal testimony of European travellers like Captain Cook, there is always the archaeological evidence relating to a range of cultures from Minoan Crete (c.2500 BC) to the Anasazi of the American Southwest (c.AD 1000), along with authenticated anthropological observation of peoples from Paraguay to Melanesia, as well as cultic groups in India and China.

FROM DEATH INTO LIFE

The religious justification for such practices varies according to time and place, but it generally seems to come down to the same underlying premise. Whether consciously or not, cannibalism seems to derive its ritual value from the way it makes death feed (quite literally) back into life. In that respect, it is comparable to headhunting – and, incidentally, as a converse to the rites of sacrifice discussed earlier, in which the blood of the living nourishes the dead.

The idea that life and fertility flow from death has been central to many religious and cultural traditions – it can be seen as underpinning those of the Christian West. In this, Christ the Redeemer makes himself the sacrifice at the crucifixion, his blood watering the earth of Mount Calvary. (From the wound made in his side by the spear of the Roman soldier, water actually streams along with blood, we are told: John XIX, 34.) And, as irreverent scholars have gleefully pointed out, Christianity makes its own oblique reference to the idea of cannibalism in the consumption of Christ's body and blood in the sacrament of the Eucharist.

The dead make many demands on us. If, in the end, we do our best to meet them, it is because we hope that death will bring us life. We want that for our own souls but also for the wider societies that we inhabit, and which inhabit us, giving us our sense of who we are. The cycle of life, death, burial and rebirth is one of the great continuities of cultural existence, as central as the growing cycle with which it is analogous. This is the hold the dead have over us. Neglect them, and we reject ourselves, giving up on the hope of any life, any meaning beyond the present moment.

Left: Blood sacrifice? The idea seems irredeemably 'primitive' to the modern mind, but it underpins the entire concept of Christian redemption.

137

138

chapter 6

TOWARDS MODERNITY, THE WESTERN TRADITION

It was in around 1448 that the German printer Johannes Gutenberg transformed his trade with the introduction of movable type. Previously, every page had needed to be carved out completely in a wooden template before it could be printed: now the text could be assembled from individual letters, cast in metal. Once the page was ready, as many copies as were required could be printed off and then the type could be broken up again to be re-used. The consequences of what is rightly called the 'Gutenberg Revolution' were far-reaching. From being the preserve of a scholarly elite, the printed word began to reach a much wider reading public. The reverberations of this change were to have an impact on every aspect of late-medieval life, and one of the first things to be affected was late-medieval death.

Left: Gutenberg's printing press famously revolutionized life in the late-Middle Ages. But its effect on death was to be just as dramatic.

'INTO THY HANDS...'

As we have seen, mortality was much on the mind of a fifteenth-century Europe, which was still reeling from the effects of the Black Death. Hence the grim enthusiasm that greeted the publication of the book that became generally known as *Ars moriendi* ('The Art of Dying'). Essentially a 'how-to' guide to death, it offered consoling thoughts of salvation on the one hand and, on the other, forthright points about how the dying might be prepared for the coming Judgment. There were tips on how their loved ones might help them to manage their fears and temptations, and prayers that might be offered on their behalf. The book was originally written around 1415, by an unknown Dominican friar, and this version had been widely copied. Some time around 1450, a shortened version appeared, which was printed the old-fashioned way, from wood-blocks, with engraved illustrations. These same illustrations were used in the movable-type versions that followed in the 1460s. By century's end, there would have been almost a hundred editions.

The *Ars moriendi* was not just a publishing phenomenon – it represented a major concession by the Church. For it effectively gave families a spiritual stewardship over their loved ones, which would previously have been regarded as being the prerogative of the priest. This made sense, given the way the ranks of the Church had been cut down during the Black Death, but it may also be seen as helping to advance that increase in ecclesiastical 'people power' that was ultimately to lead to Reformation. The main impact of Protestantism, when it came, would be to sweep away the barriers Catholicism had erected between individual Christians and their God. The institutional hierarchy was slashed and the scriptures translated into the vernacular languages, so that ordinary men and women might have access to the divine Word.

Death was also something that Christians knew they would finally have to face alone, though the family had its part to play. So too, for the moment, did the Church: while much of their earlier advice and support was now available in book form, priests still had a special place as ministers of the Extreme Unction or the Sacrament of the Sick. Also known as the Last Sacrament, this was the final anointment with holy oil that assured the dying the best possible send-off into the beyond. It was an enormous comfort to those who found themselves facing death. Be that as it may, however, there had overall been a devolution of rights over the whole business of dying from the institutions of the Church to the family and the individual. With rights came responsibilities: death was in some ways even scarier for those who knew that their salvation or damnation now lay in their own hands. On the whole, though, the changes were empowering for those respectable folk whose lives were orderly and well-regulated and who could feel they were taking charge of their preparations for a 'good death'.

> There were tips on how their loved ones might help them to manage their fears and temptations, and prayers that might be offered on their behalf.

AT THE HEART OF THE COMMUNITY

The English poet Thomas Gray, who died in 1771, is buried in the little churchyard at Stoke Poges, Buckinghamshire, UK. It is here that he is believed to have written his most famous work. For many, indeed, his 'Elegy, Written in a Country Churchyard' captures something quintessential and timeless in English life. It is certainly atmospheric:

The Curfew tolls the knell of parting day,
The lowing herd wind slowly o'er the lea,
The plowman homeward plods his weary way,
And leaves the world to darkness, and to me.

Now fades the glimmering landscape on the sight,
And all the air a solemn stillness holds,
Save where the beetle wheels its droning flight,
And drowsy tinklings lull the distant folds;

Save that from yonder ivy-mantled tow'r,
The mopeing owl doth to the moon complain
Of such as, wand'ring near her sacred bow'r
Molest her ancient, solitary reign.

Above: Thomas Gray's 'Elegy, Written in a Country Churchyard' made mortality seem comfortable, almost cosy. The churchyard in question was this one at Stoke Poges, Berkshire.

The mood is one of peace; there is nothing disconcerting about the onset of night. This is no place of vampires, ghosts or ghouls. Far from being troubled, Gray is reassured by the presence of the dead, the source of a companionable peace:

Beneath those rugged elms, that yew-tree's shade,
Where heaves the earth in many a mould'ring heap,

> Each in his narrow cell forever laid,
> The rude forefathers of the hamlet sleep.

An idealizing view, of course, and certainly not 'timeless' – in the Middle Ages, poor villagers had seldom been left to sleep undisturbed, but were buried in shallow graves so that their bones could be dug up and tossed into charnel houses once their flesh had decayed. Not until the sixteenth century did even relatively prominent villagers have permanent graves. By Gray's time, however, the churchyard had indeed developed into a focal point of village life. The poet puts his finger on the way that the churchyard was now at the very heart of the early-modern village, in a way that – now more than ever – seems to be somehow quintessentially 'English'.

There are good reasons why this should be so. First, the succession of generations is clearly on display in such places, in a way that it cannot be in a modern city cemetery, and this drives home the feeling of continuity. Then there is the clear sense we get of social cohesiveness, something else for which we may be tempted to look back nostalgically to the past. **Not that there was any absence of hierarchy in death: the local aristocracy typically had tombs within the church, or vaults beneath it;** the gentry were buried in the aisles and had memorial tablets in the walls nearby. Of those outside, the more prosperous took the places nearer the door. Yet, for all that, we still have the feeling that the whole village is together here, a close-knit community in death just as in life. However grim the reality of rural life for the vast majority of those forced to live it, this village vision cannot help but seem idyllic to those who feel uprooted and adrift in a modern society in which mass media, big corporations and impersonal bureaucracies apparently hold sway.

The way in which death's rituals might unite all is clear from the will left by the Hampshire naturalist, Thomas White of Selborne. He died in 1793, having expressed the wish to be buried

> ...in the church yard belonging to the parish church of Selborne aforesaid in as plain and private a way as possible without any pall bearers or parade and that six honest day labouring men respect being had to such as have bred up large families may bear me to my grave.

It is worth remembering that the fee for this job would have made an appreciable difference to a poor family's income. With this request, White is determined to do his social duty to the last.

In the church at Hertingfordbury, Hertfordshire, certificates can be seen relating to an ordinance of eighteenth-century law. This provided that, as a protectionist measure to assist the local textile industry, the dead had to be buried in woollen shrouds. 'To make these dresses is a particular trade,' observed a French visitor, Monsieur Misson, 'and there are many that sell nothing else; so that these habits for the dead are always to be had ready-made, of what size or price you please, for people of every age and sex.'

But there were far stranger ways in which death might favour the 'trickling down' of prosperity from the wealthy to the poor in the rustic economy, as diarist John Evelyn was to report in the seventeenth century:

In the county of Hereford was an old custom at funerals, to hire poor people, who were to take upon them all the sins of the party deceased. One of them I remember (he was a long, lean, lamentable, poor rascal) lived in a cottage on Ross highway. The manner was that when the corpse was brought out of the house and laid on the bier, a loaf of bread was brought out, and delivered to the sin-eater over the corpse, as also a mazard [cherry] bowl full of beer, which he was to drink up, and sixpence in money, in consideration whereof he took upon him...all the sins of the defunct, and freed him or her from walking after they were dead.

Left: Graveyards in the colonies took on a special significance, representing 'rootedness', continuity, in a new and foreign land.

Above: When plague epidemics raged, the ritual niceties had to be abandoned – bodies were heaped into carts and dumped in pits.

English colonists took their traditions with them when they went to North America. Here too a death was experienced as a communal event. As soon as he heard the news of a person's passing, the town sexton tolled the bell: nine chimes for a man, six for a woman and three for a child. And then came further chimes: one for each year of the dead person's life. Those listening at home could generally guess who had died. Neighbours gathered at the house to comfort the bereaved and help with laying out the corpse – washing it, trimming untidy hair and, if an adult male, giving it a final shave. Not until the early nineteenth century did such services start to be professionalized, and even then it was only in the cities. A shroud of cotton or linen was made: it had sleeves but was open at the back. The poor would simply be wrapped in a 'winding sheet'. There was no embalming, so time was pressing, and shrouds from this period show signs of having been tacked together fairly hastily. Soft pine wood was used for coffins, again for speed.

The body was typically displayed overnight in the best room in the house before burial. Those of Scotch-Irish ancestry held wakes, which sometimes grew rowdy. The whole town would turn out to see the coffin borne solemnly to the graveyard. 'Funerals', recalled Horace Greeley of his New England childhood in the early nineteenth century, 'were attended by nearly every one who seasonally heard of them.'

It shocked white Americans – and, frankly, frightened them – that slaves held their funerals at night, singing loudly as they bore the deceased to the grave by the flickering light of torches. While this practice no doubt reflected the different customs, traditions and attitudes that they had brought with them from Africa, it stemmed too from the fact that the hours of darkness were the only ones in which they had any degree of autonomy.

EMERGENCY MEASURES

Back in England, meanwhile, the idyll had long since ended for most, especially in the urban centres. As time went on and the population rose, churchyards were filled to bursting, with the results that John Evelyn had noted in Norwich as early as the seventeenth century:

> Most of the Church-yards (though some of them large enough) were filled up with earth, or rather the congestion of dead bodies one upon another, for want of Earth etc to the very top of the Walls, and many above the walls, so as the Churches seem'd to be built in pitts.

Congestion gave way to crisis when, in 1665, a plague epidemic erupted: the last and most severe of the epidemiological aftershocks of the Black Death of the fourteenth century. The funerary infrastructure of London, in particular, was overloaded. As other leading citizens fled, clergyman Dr Thomas Vincent stayed in the capital, to witness:

> Multitudes, multitudes, in the valley of the shadow of death thronging daily into Eternity; the Churchyards now are stuft so full with dead corpses, that they are in many places swell'd two or three foot higher than they were before, and new ground is broken up to bury the dead.

Daniel Defoe's *A Journal of the Plague Year* was published in 1722, more than half a century after the events it describes, but was so meticulously researched and vividly written as to read like first-hand testimony. No churchyard idyll was available to those who fell victim to this dreadful pestilence, wrote the author of *Robinson Crusoe:*

> The cart had in it sixteen or seventeen bodies; some were wrapt up in linen sheets, some in rags, some little other than naked or so loose that what covering they had fell from them in the shooting out of the cart, and they fell quite naked among the rest; but the matter was not much to them, or the indecency much to any one else, seeing they were all dead, and were to be huddled together in to the common grave of mankind, as we may call it, for here was no difference made, but poor and rich went together; there was no other way of burials, neither was it possible there should be, for coffins were not to be had for the prodigious numbers that fell in such a calamity as this.

Mass graves became the norm, but even these could barely be dug quickly enough. Defoe writes of one vast trench at Aldgate:

As soon as he heard the news of a person's passing, the town sexton tolled the bell: nine chimes for a man, six for a woman and three for a child.

145

They had supposed this pit would have supplied them for a month or more when they dug it, and some blamed the churchwardens for suffering such – frightful thing, telling them they were making preparations to bury the whole parish, and the like; but time made it appear the churchwardens knew the condition of the parish better than they did: for, the pit being finished the 4th of September, I think, they began to bury in it the 6th, and by the 20th, which was just two weeks, they had thrown into it 1114 bodies.

The passing of the plague meant that the population quickly recovered, to grow apace throughout the eighteenth century. By the 1840s, indeed, physician Sir John Simon was alerting a parliamentary committee to what he saw as the health hazard that London's overcrowded churches represented:

It is a very serious matter that beneath the feet of those who attend the services of their church, there often lies an almost solid mass of decomposing human remains heaped as high as the vaulting will permit and generally but very partially confined.

Below: Dissection of the dead was seen as vital if young doctors were to learn their trade, but no one would have volunteered their body for such a use.

Outside in the churchyards it was no better: the burial-ground of St Martin-in-the-Fields covered only about 18.5 square metres (200 square feet), but was estimated to contain in the region of 70,000 bodies. There was no real prospect

of a 'decent' burial under such circumstances nor, for the poor, any pretence of that. Their coffins were lowered into deep pits, 17 or 18 at a time. That was if they even made it into the earth, for many had their coffins stolen and re-sold as firewood, while their bodies were sold for medical research.

DEATH AND DISSECTION

The late-eighteenth century saw the rise of scientific medicine, which would eventually bring great dividends for the living. Those rewards would be long in coming, though: it has been suggested that it was only in the second half of the nineteenth century that any appreciable advances were made. In the immediate term, the greatest impact was on the dead. Medical students could learn about anatomy only by the dissection of actual bodies. Especially around the main teaching centres in London and Edinburgh, the demand was growing for cadavers for dissection.

Even today, many have mixed feelings about the idea of organ donation, but in those times Christians looked forward to the resurrection of the body. What was to become of someone whose physical form had been carved up and taken apart to be shown to students, or dismembered in the cause of scientific enquiry? The very thought filled men and women with genuine dread, which was why – in theory at least – only the bodies of executed criminals were given up for dissection. But the demand far outstripped the supply afforded even by England's notorious 'Bloody Code' (which listed more than 200 capital offences, including the stealing of a sheep, cutting down trees or, for an unwed mother, concealing a stillborn child).

Little surprise, then, that 'resurrectionists' flourished. These were criminals who, under cover of darkness, entered graveyards where burials had recently taken place. Digging up these coffins, they sold the bodies to unscrupulous doctors. The rewards were great: in the late-eighteenth century, the going rate for a body was in the region of two guineas; by 1828, a parliamentary committee heard, it was more like eight. The result, inevitably, was a large-scale traffic. In 1794, for instance, the *Gentleman's Magazine* reported that:

> A hackney coachman, who was apprehended in conveying dead bodies, from the burial ground in High-Street, Lambeth, was brought before the magistrates, at Union Hall, Borough, for examination… At the time the coach was seized, the body of the late porter to the Archbishop of Canterbury, that of a young woman, and two children, were found in it. The parish having given permission to the friends of such persons as have been buried in this ground, to examine whether or not the bodies remained there, most of the graves have been opened, and, shocking to say, upwards of two hundred of coffins have been taken up empty.

New graves not only contained fresher corpses, but were easier to dig up because the earth was loose around them. The wealthy could afford heavy coffins, and increasingly, these were built for strength and security: some had double or triple caskets that were lined with lead. The poor suffered disproportionately since, being buried together in coffinless batches, and often none too deeply, they could be dug up very quickly and easily. They were only too well aware, meanwhile, that it would not be their sons and daughters who benefited from any medical advances, but those of the wealthy, who would be able to afford the doctors' fees. The suspicion grew that the Establishment was turning a blind eye to this dreadful trade.

THE RISE OF THE CEMETERY

Despite the best efforts of the resurrectionists, the city churchyards continued to overflow. The upper and middle classes became increasingly unwilling to be buried there. It was not just a question of the security or the dignity of the dead, but the danger that their families might come into contact with a lower class of mourner, risking – it was felt – not just social contamination but disease. The old inner quarters of London (as of other big cities) were now for the most part little more than pestilential slums. Wealthier citizens had already moved out to villas in leafy suburbs, so it made sense for them to be laid to rest in the various cemeteries that were being opened there. Similar problems in Paris had prompted Napoleon to found Père Lachaise cemetery: this had become so fashionable that it was almost worth dying to gain entry.

In London, Kensal Green's success spurred other entrepreneurs to start their own cemeteries.

Kensal Green, opened in 1833 and thus the first of London's major cemeteries, became known as 'the Belgravia of Death', after London's most exclusive neighbourhood. It was run strictly on business lines, but it catered for a class of consumers that was ready to pay extra for something a cut above the average. In Kensal Green, there was space and scope for the sort of grandiose monuments that came into fashion as the wealthy started to die with style. There was space also for sweeping avenues and roadways so that hearses and carriages could come right to the graveside. Here were classical colonnades, and chapels with catacombs. If there was anything unseemly about running a graveyard on a commercial basis, this had never held back the clergy – the opening of London's Kensal Green cemetery is believed to have cost the parish of Paddington some £200 a year in burial fees. And while an earlier age might have jibbed at not being buried in 'God's Acre', on 'hallowed ground', the actual squalor of these churchyards seemed to make a nonsense of such scruples.

Glasgow's great Necropolis, opened just a few weeks after Kensal Green, was also very much run on a commercial basis. With its spectacular hilltop setting, it is perhaps the most beautiful of Britain's Victorian cemeteries. Its founders' stated aim was to 'afford a much wanted accommodation to the higher classes [and] convert an unproductive property into a general and lucrative source of profit.' The cemetery would be non-denominational. Plots were to be 5m (16ft) broad (quite unthinkable in any of the city churchyards) and the grounds were to be well-maintained, under the supervision of a gardener. The company would have approval of any memorials proposed. There were different charges for burial plots in different parts of the cemetery – so the Necropolis had its own social hierarchy, just as in Glasgow itself. But those with the money could go to their graves here in the confidence that this last resting place would be fittingly salubrious. A sliding scale of charges governed the cost of funerals, depending on whether the coffin was borne on a four-horse or two-horse hearse, or on a handcart, with or without ushers. The new cemeteries, writes Ronnie Scott, offered not just a great deal more space, but a new aesthetic, a new sensibility, founded in the values of the European Enlightenment. The macabre and the grim were banished from their precincts: 'This new, enlightened approach to death and the hereafter…was thought of as a long sleep rather than as an eternity of terrors'. Gone were the skulls and dances of death, to be replaced by 'more cheerful symbols of resurrection and eternal life':

> The winged soul, ascending to heaven; the Angel of the Resurrection, holding or blowing trumpets; the Radiance, represented by clouds, the sun, sunrays, trumpets or a sunburst; a flaming heart; palm fronds; an anchor; the Holy Spirit in the form of a dove; statues or carvings of Faith, Hope and Charity …

With medieval iconography went every trace of the gothic style, to be replaced by a sober yet un-scary neo-classicism.

In London, Kensal Green's success spurred other entrepreneurs to start their own cemeteries. Norwood followed in 1837, Highgate in 1839 and Abney Park, Brompton and Nunhead in 1840. Yet in scale at least, all these were eclipsed by Brookwood, outside Woking, founded by the Necropolis and National Mausoleum Company and opened in 1854. The new super-cemetery sprawled over 800 hectares (2000 acres) of Surrey countryside – enough, it was thought,

Left: If immortality was out of the question, Londoners could still aspire to spend eternity in the elegant surroundings of Kensal Green.

Above: The Victorians built cemeteries on a scale and of an elaborateness not seen since Etruscan times: this one is at Highgate, in north London.

to house all of London's dead for as long as could possibly be envisaged. It had its own purpose-built rail link to the capital, with regular services from Waterloo Station, both for funeral parties and for relatives visiting graves.

DEATH AS SPECTACLE

Kensal Green was a success from the start, but it is generally considered to have 'come of age' with the interment of August Frederick, Duke of Sussex, in 1843. A son of King George III, his splendid funeral here placed the cemetery very firmly on the map of fashion. This was an age of great state funerals. In January 1806, there had been an inspirational farewell for Admiral Lord Nelson, after his dramatic death in the hour of victory at Trafalgar (1805). His body, brought home in a barrel of brandy and pure alcohol, lay in state in the Painted Hall at Greenwich Hospital. In the space of three days, an estimated 30,000 people came to view the body in its coffin: so great were the crowds that the authorities feared a riot. Then, appropriately enough for a man of the sea, the late admiral was borne upriver to central London in a grand procession of barges, all richly decorated. The barge that carried Nelson had once belonged to King Charles II; now it was draped with black velvet and displayed waving black ostrich plumes. Kept overnight at the Admiralty in Whitehall, the body was then loaded on to a carriage made to look like his late flagship, HMS *Victory,* for the journey to St Paul's Cathedral, through streets crammed with silent crowds, all dressed in the black of mourning. The procession was enormous: so long that when the advance guard reached St Paul's, the rear had yet to leave Whitehall. The astonishing hearse apart, what stole the show was the sight of the crew of the *Victory*, who between them bore the ship's colours, now tattered by the shot of battle. The organizers had not wanted to include these lowly mourners, but had been more or less forced into it by the popular press – this funeral was very much a 'media event'.

Inside St Paul's, its vast dome illuminated for the occasion with lamps hung from on high, the coffin was placed on a high catafalque or platform. As a short and simple service concluded, it began to sink slowly through the floor and out of sight into the crypt, where Nelson was to have his permanent tomb. Rather than placing the *Victory*'s ensign reverently aside, the admiral's crewmen now tore it into shreds for souvenirs. It was just the sort of outrage against protocol that the Admiralty had presumably feared when they first refused to give these

Below: Nelson's funeral car reaches St Paul's cathedral for the climax of a ceremony which was at once an act of mourning and a celebration of victory.

Right: Nelson's final resting-place, in the crypt at St Paul's, became a place of patriotic pilgrimage. Eventually he would be joined by the Duke of Wellington.

Right: Nelson's final resting-place, in the crypt at St Paul's, became a place of patriotic pilgrimage. Eventually he would be joined by the Duke of Wellington.

sailors a part in the ceremony. Far from giving offence, however, it merely underlined for the leading mourners the adulation that the dead man had been accorded by the ordinary people.

Forty-six years later, it was to be the turn of the Duke of Wellington, Britain's commander at the Battle of Waterloo (1815), and later Prime Minister. He died at his home, Walmer Castle in Kent, and was then taken to London to lie in state at the Chelsea Hospital, a home for veterans in the west of the capital. Queen Victoria was among the first to pay her respects, and was overcome by emotion at the death of the man she regarded as the saviour of his nation. The people agreed with her estimation and, once the doors were thrown open for the public, the crowds arriving on foot and by carriage caused congestion for miles around. Once again, people grew agitated, fearing that they would not get to see the hero, and two women were crushed to death in the resulting press. On the day of the funeral, 18 November 1852, the 'Iron Duke' was placed on his funeral car, a 12-ton hearse festooned with black banners and ostrich feathers and drawn by 12 black horses, with black plumes on their heads. For *The Times*, this car was:

> By far the most magnificent and interesting part of the procession. The whole lower part is of bronze. Above this rises a rich pediment of gilding, with a list of victories inscribed. On the sides, lofty coats of arms are surmounted by Ducal coronets and batons, topped by a velvet pall, embroidered with laurels in silver and the legend 'Blessed are the Dead that die in the Lord'.

The army was also, naturally, out in force: every regiment was represented, either in the cortège or as an honour-guard along the processional route. Behind them, the streets were thronged by a solemn but excited crowd, many thousands in number. Rooftops and balconies overlooking the route were filled with onlookers, and people even paid to stand in shop windows from where they could look over the heads of the people on the pavements.

This was death as both national event and national presentation, a performance consciously managed – even concocted, one might say. While clearly in no doubt about the sincerity of the people's grief, the *Illustrated London News* is frank about the element of staginess in the ceremonial, but then goes on to praise the thoughtfulness and skill with which the whole event was put together:

> All that ingenuity could suggest in the funeral trappings, all that imagination and fancy could devise to surround the ceremonial with accessories that most forcibly impress the minds of a multitude, all the grace that Royalty could lend, all the aid that the State could afford in every one of its great departments, all the imposing circumstances derivable from the assemblage of great masses of men arrayed with military splendour and in military mourning, together with the less dramatic but even more affecting grief expressed by the sober trappings of respectful and sympathetic crowds, all the dignity that could be conferred by the presence of the civil and legislative power of a great and ancient kingdom; and, lastly, all the sanctity and awe inspired by the grandest of religious services performed in the grandest Protestant temple in the world, were combined to render the scene inside and outside of St Paul's Cathedral...the most memorable in our annals.

'The Hero sleeps well,' the paper concluded, rousingly:

> May we never miss in a future day the guiding hand and the clear judgement of him who gave nearly forty years' peace to Europe, who was the benefactor of every kingdom in it... No Caesar ever approached such deeds as these; and all Greek and Roman fame are but small and mean compared with the pure fame of the GREAT DUKE OF WELLINGTON!

The implication would have been clear to readers: if the Iron Duke's achievements topped those of the ancient heroes, his country's glory was greater than that of either Greece or Rome. In mourning the one, Britons were celebrating the other: this was a moment of the utmost patriotic fervour.

Yet, even as it proclaimed the national significance of Wellington's death, the *Illustrated London News* was at pains to insist upon the private tragedy. Readers were invited to witness the 'Last Moments' of the dead man in a manner that now seems at once cloyingly over-reverential and startlingly intrusive:

> On Tuesday morning, September 14, the Duke of Wellington complained of uneasiness in the chest and stomach. At this time there were no symptoms indicative of danger, but shortly his Grace became much worse, became unconscious and breathed laboriously. Remedial measures which in former attacks had been useful were now of no avail. Shortly after one o'clock he

Queen Victoria was among the first to pay her respects, and she was overcome by emotion at the death of the man she regarded as the saviour of his nation.

153

became very restless – the eye glassy. Respiration became very difficult, but easier when his Grace was placed in an easy chair; but the pulse sank and at twenty-five minutes past three o'clock p.m. his Grace expired.

As if that description were not enough, readers were even given an account of 'The Room at Walmer Castle':

The room in which the Duke expired is of moderate size and plainly furnished: but everything neatly and methodically arranged something like an officer's room in a garrison. On the right-hand side stands an ordinary iron camp bedstead, with a single horse-hair mattress, and a horse-hair pillow covered with leather, which the Duke usually carried with him and used in town. Summer or winter the little camp bedstead was without curtains. Here the Duke always slept and wrote, when at Walmer. Over the bedstead is a small collection of books, evidently selected for use… In the centre of the room is a mahogany table, well stained with ink, and

Right: Mourning became Queen Victoria – or at least it became her trademark after the death of her Prince Consort, Albert, in 1861.

covered with papers; and here for some hours every day the Duke sat and wrote. Near this is a more portable one, and contrived so as to be used for reading and writing while in bed. This, with two or three chairs, comprises the whole.

While the military virtues are emphasized here – the austere simplicity in which the Duke had lived – the article has something of the flavour of today's celebrity lifestyle magazines. Like the medieval pilgrim pushing into the 'squeezing place' (*see* Chapter 4), people wanted to get as close as they could to the great man: journalism of this sort allowed them to do that 'virtually'.

PRIVATE GRIEF IN PUBLIC

Prince Albert, Queen Victoria's Consort, died nine years later, in 1861. He had requested a simple, private ceremony. His death impacted on the nation, though, his widow effectively withdrawing from public life, wearing black and allowing herself to be defined by her grief for many years afterwards. In time, her extended mourning came to seem excessive to most of her subjects, and there were even mutterings that she was shirking her responsibilities as monarch. But hers is only an extreme example of a Victorian mourning culture in which private grief came to be seen as a public duty.

It is quite possible, indeed, that Victoria's reaction to her husband's death was an important factor in making mourning 'fashionable'. For working-class women, life had to go on, with the household to be run and a living to be made, but they were expected to wear black and bear themselves with unimpeachable modesty for a lengthy period. Middle- and upper-class wives, however, always walking advertisements for their husbands' prosperity and taste, had much the same responsibility in widowhood. The widow of good family had to go into deep mourning for a year. She wore black crêpe, barely ventured out, and went veiled when she did so, her cloak often trimmed with an edging of black fur. Though this strict code would eventually ease, it did so only by slow degrees. Historian Catharine Arnold describes the appointed stages:

> Once a widow had completed her first year, she dressed in 'secondary mourning'. This had a less rigorous dress code, and white collars and cuffs, reminiscent of a nun's habit, were permitted. After nine months came 'ordinary mourning', a three-month stretch during which women were permitted to wear shiny fabrics such as silk and velvet, trimmed with lace or beads, and also gold and silver jewellery, with appropriately sombre precious stones like amethysts, garnets and opals. Finally, a widow entered the six months of 'half-mourning', when muted colours such as grey, purple and lilac were permissible. Black evening dress was accessorized with a black fan, trimmed with ostrich feathers, and, should she be deaf, a black Vulcanite mourning ear trumpet.

With so many different 'looks' to be captured at the various stages of mourning… bereavement became a branch of consumerism.

With so many 'looks' to be captured at the various stages of mourning, without any loss of individuality or lapse in taste, bereavement became a branch of consumerism. Specialized dressmakers, manufacturers, retailers, advertisers and magazine publishers gained as much as undertakers from the business of death.

Not that the undertakers did so badly. Enormous social pressures were brought to bear to make sure that families 'did the right thing by' their deceased.

155

'Many individuals', Arnold points out, 'had more money spent on them dead than alive.' She gives two examples of the sorts of funerals on offer. The first, costing £4, 14 shillings, involved:

> Hearse and pair of horses; a mourning coach and pair; fifteen plumes of black ostrich-feathers, and complete velvet covering for carriages and horses; stout elm coffin, with inner lid, covered with black cloth, set with two rows all round of best black nails; lead plate of inscription, lid ornaments, four pairs of handles and grips, all of the best improved jet and bright black; tufted mattress, lined and ruffled, and fine cambric winding-sheet; use of silk velvet pall; two mutes with 2 gowns, silk hatbands, and gloves, eight men as pages and coachmen, with truncheons and wands, crêpe hatbands, &c.

This respectable but modest funeral would suit a lower-middle-class family, though they might well find themselves crippled by the cost. But only the very wealthy could conceive of springing £53 on a funeral such as this:

> Hearse and four horses, two mourning coaches with fours, twenty-three plumes of rich ostrich feathers, complete velvet covering for carriages and horses, and an esquire's plume of best feathers; strong elm shell, with tufted mattress, lined and ruffled with superfine cambric, and pillow; full worked glazed cambric winding-sheet, stout outside lead coffin, with inscription plate and solder complete; one and a half inch oak case, covered with black or crimson velvet, set with three rows round, and lid panelled with best brass nails; stout brass plate of inscription, richly engraved four pairs of best brass handles and grips, lid ornaments to correspond; use of silk velvet pall; two mutes with gowns, silk hatbands and gloves; fourteen men as pages, feathermen, and coachmen, with truncheons and wands, silk hatbands &c; use of mourners' fittings; and attendant with silk hatband &c.

The cheapest funeral offered by this particular firm cost £3, 5 shillings: yet even this was far beyond the reach of many at the time. People saved if they possibly could ('Friendly Societies' and savings banks boomed through this period), but many were reduced to dying 'on the parish'.

In a society whose highest value was 'self-help', there was contempt for those who died destitute in the workhouses or the slums, and no attempt was made to ease the humiliation for their families. Karl Marx's collaborator, Friedrich Engels, was – not surprisingly – unimpressed:

> In death as in life, the poor in England are treated in an utterly shameless manner. Their corpses have no better fate than the carcasses of animals. The pauper burial ground at St Bride's in London is an open piece of marshland which has been used since Charles II's day and there are heaps of bones all over the place. Every Wednesday the remains of dead paupers are thrown into a hole which is fourteen feet deep. A clergyman gabbles through the burial service and then the grave is filled with loose soil. On the following Wednesday the ground is opened again and this goes on until it is completely full. The whole neighbourhood is infected by the dreadful stench from this burial ground.

IN LOVING MEMORY
OF

Edward Field.

Who departed this life October 24th, 1914,

AGED 48 YEARS.

Interred at Islington Cemetery, Finchley, Church Ground

October 29th, 1914.   Grave No. 70017.   Block O.

Gone from us but not forgotten,
Never shall thy memory fade ;
Sweetest thoughts shall ever linger,
Round the spot where thou art laid.

P. Knowland, Undertaker, 19, Murray Street, New North Road, N.
and 45, Bevenden Street, East Road, Hoxton, N.

Left: A strict etiquette came to govern mourning in the Victorian period. This funeral card was designed to be kept in the home as a memorial to the deceased.

As late as 1911, Robert Noonan, the author of the classic socialist novel *The Ragged-Trousered Philanthropists,* published under the pen-name of Robert Tressell, was buried at what was then the Walton Workhouse (now a prison) in Liverpool. He was laid to rest in a pauper's grave along with 12 other men and women, their grave only recently marked with a memorial.

'THE AMERICAN WAY OF DEATH'

In many respects, the United States followed unfolding trends in Britain and Europe, especially in the big cities of the East. An increasingly professionalized funeral industry took charge of tasks once shared by neighbouring women, and extravagant shows of mourning were required. Yet since the Civil War of 1861–65, America had been taking its own direction in important ways. This

terrible conflict, which changed so much in American society, had a lasting influence on the culture of death.

More than half a million lives were lost in the Civil War, which produced a great many grieving relatives, their homes often at some considerable distance from the battlefields. They ached to see the bodies of their loved ones before they were laid to rest, a facility for which some of them were able and willing to pay. Hence the re-entrance of the embalmer into funerary history: men with the knowledge and the skills to hold back the process of decay. The odd European monarch apart, embalming had fallen out of use centuries before; indeed, most Americans now found the idea disturbingly macabre. But the promise of being able to see the dead before they were buried helped to conquer such resistance, and in the decades that followed, the embalmers forced their way into the funerary mainstream.

On the one hand, they promoted embalming as a modern 'science', calling themselves 'morticians'; on the other, they drew attention to the antiquity of the 'art'. It was expensive, this could not be denied, but surely you would not begrudge a beloved parent, spouse or child a treatment that would ensure they stayed physically intact? The fashion – encouraged by the industry – for an open coffin at the funeral obviously ensured that the appearance of the body became a real issue. And the more professionalized the service, the more squeamish consumers inevitably became. Americans whose grandmothers had been content to sew shrouds for bodies laid out in the family parlour now wished to see only a perfect simulacrum of the living person. By the beginning of the twentieth century, that transformation was more or less complete: no normal family would even think of taking on such responsibilities itself. The presence of death would contaminate the family house, it was felt, so the body would instead rest in the 'funeral home' until, having been rendered pristine by the embalmers, it was ready to be laid in earth.

It was partly, perhaps, as a result of such feelings of 'denial' that the 'lawn cemetery' became fashionable in the late-nineteenth century. In beautifully landscaped parklands, the graves seemed almost incidental, their markers deliberately discreet. Certainly, they were not allowed to disrupt the vista – there were no big statues or built-up tombs, no railings to mark off one plot from another, no regimented ranks of graves. Visitors could almost forget that they were standing in a cemetery. This, of course, was very much the point.

From the first, the growing role of the funerary business was not without its critics. Many argued that it was little more than a heartless racket. Such dissent grew as the industry itself did, through the twentieth century. Countless Americans did have reservations about the system, but it would take the intervention of two English outsiders to place the activities of the undertakers in the spotlight. In 1948, Evelyn Waugh published a satirical novel on the subject, *The Loved One,* and this was followed in 1963 by Jessica Mitford's *The American Way of Death*. The latter was a witty and hugely entertaining book, but its humour did nothing to disguise what the Englishwoman considered to be the cynicism of an industry that preyed on ordinary families at their most vulnerable. Its aggressive marketing shaded over into moral blackmail and bullying, said Mitford; its charges were grossly inflated and many of its claims were, frankly, false.

Left: Increasingly uncomfortable with the idea of death, Americans took with enthusiasm to the new 'lawn cemeteries' like the famous one at Forest Lawn, Glendale, Los Angeles.

The presence of death would contaminate the family house, it was felt, so the body would instead rest in the 'funeral home' until, rendered pristine by the embalmers, it was ready to be laid in earth.

Right: Jessica Mitford caused a stir with her mischievous observations on the 'American Way of Death', but many of her criticisms were well-founded.

There was much truth in these allegations. Many Americans were, to put it no more strongly than this, allowed to believe that the expensive embalming process was a requirement of US law. Some seem to have been persuaded, moreover, that it would preserve the body in perpetuity, whereas the reality is that it can preserve the body only through to the funeral.

Today, the practice of embalmment continues to be a controversial question. As traditional religious reservations have weakened, the industry has increasingly resorted to psychological arguments to defend the practice. The 'last look' at the loved one is, according to the industry, a crucial part of the 'grieving process', so it is therefore important that the body should be intact to save distress. Good pscyhology, or mere pscyhobabble?

At the same time, it seems only fair to point out that Mitford was writing at the very height of post-war consumerism in America. This was a time when the manufacturing industry was providing more and bigger cars, refrigerators and all sorts of other items – and a vast and resourceful advertising and sales sector had grown up to help convince people of the 'need' for these items. That people were also being pressed into purchasing bigger funerals than ever before is hardly surprising, then, and it seems unfair to single out the undertakers for special censure. It is still interesting, however, to see the extent to which consumerism had by now encroached on areas that had once been (and in theory were still) held 'sacred', off-limits to commerce.

GRAVES FIT FOR HEROES

The American Civil War has often been described as the first modern war, for the use of heavy artillery and automatic weapons allowed mass slaughter on an unprecedented scale. Almost 8000 soldiers fell at Gettysburg, Pennsylvania, on 13 July 1863. Though the remains of some were embalmed and shipped home, many ended up being buried close to where they had fallen, in what is now the Gettysburg National Cemetery. It was dedicated just a few months after the battle, on 19 November, in a ceremony at which President Abraham Lincoln made his famous Gettysburg Address:

> Four score and seven years ago our fathers brought forth on this continent a new nation, conceived in Liberty, and dedicated to the proposition that all men are created equal.
>
> Now we are engaged in a great civil war, testing whether that nation, or any nation, so conceived and so dedicated, can long endure. We are met on a great battle-field of that war. We have come to dedicate a portion of that field, as a final

Left: There can only be numbers for the unknown dead interred in the Gettysburg National Cemetery, Pennsylvania, but these have a poignancy all their own.

161

resting place for those who here gave their lives that that nation might live. It is altogether fitting and proper that we should do this.

But, in a larger sense, we can not dedicate – we can not consecrate – we can not hallow – this ground. The brave men, living and dead, who struggled here, have consecrated it, far above our poor power to add or detract. The world will little note, nor long remember what we say here, but it can never forget what they did here. It is for us the living, rather, to be dedicated here to the unfinished work which they who fought here have thus far so nobly advanced ... that this nation, under God, shall have a new birth of freedom – and that government of the people, by the people, for the people, shall not perish from the earth.

An ancient rhetoric of death and rebirth is dusted off – and given a more modern take, the sacrifice of the dead being seen as so many votes for democracy. That many had fought for the Southern, Confederate side, against Lincoln's Republican reformism, mattered nothing in the President's vision of federal brotherhood and national healing.

Yet it could certainly be argued that the Civil War had made America a better place. Few have tried to make that claim for World War I (1914–18). Over eight million troops (and more than six million civilians) were to be killed in the conflict as a whole – Britain lost 19,240 men in a single day during the Battle of the Somme. Large areas of northern France are now given over to military cemeteries, white crosses covering the rolling countryside. The famous Flanders poppies, red and beautiful as life, yet so easily snapped off at the stem, have become a major part of Britain's iconography of military mourning.

By the time of World War II (1939–45), military tactics had moved on. The conflict was fought over a vast area, with comparatively few pitched battles. But at Colleville-sur-Mer in Normandy, overlooking what was codenamed Omaha Beach for the D-Day Landings of 1944, 9387 dead US servicemen were buried in a military cemetery. For the many aviators lost in far distant lands and seamen lost at sea, there could generally be nothing more than memorials at home. At Pearl Harbor, however, where 1177 men aboard the USS *Arizona* were lost when their battleship went down in the Japanese attack of 7 December 1941, a shrine has been built above the wreckage of the sunken ship. Most of their bodies were never recovered, so the wreck remains a war grave. Oil still seeps from the *Arizona*'s tanks and floats to the surface – 'black tears', some say. Sailors man the rails in respect as their vessels pass, in what is still a very busy naval base.

Heroes of a different sort were executed by the British in the aftermath of the Easter Rising in Dublin, 1916. 'A terrible beauty is born,' the poet W.B. Yeats was later to write, recycling once again the imagery of death and rebirth. But the authorities were only too mindful of the danger that the dead rebels might take on an uncontrollable new life as martyrs and that their graves might become shrines for an increasingly angry nationalism. Padraic Pearse, one of the leaders of the rising, gave a famous speech to much this effect some years before at the burial of Geremiah O'Donovan Rossa, leader of the Fenians, the nineteenth-century nationalist-revolutionary group:

Life springs from death and from the graves of patriot men and women spring living nations. The Defenders of this Realm have worked well in secret and in the open.

They think that they have purchased half of us and intimidated the other half. They think that they have foreseen everything, they think they have provided against everything; but the fools, the fools, they have left us our Fenian dead, and while Ireland holds these graves Ireland unfree shall never be at peace.

Above: Sailors still salute as their vessels pass the sunken remains of the USS Arizona, in Pearl Harbor, now both a war-grave and a national shrine.

It was for such reasons that the British buried the dead men out of public reach in a yard at their barracks at Arbour Hill, throwing quicklime – a strongly alkaline powder of calcium oxide – into their grave to corrode away the bodies. It was a strategy that backfired. By refusing the dead a shrine and thus denying the importance of the rising, by refusing a sense of what would now be called 'closure', the spirit of rebellion only seemed to rage the more fiercely in Ireland.

UP IN SMOKE

It was in 1884 that, on the top of a hill in a South Wales field, Dr William Price of Llantrisant set light to modern Britain's first funeral pyre. On it burned his baby son. Price narrowly escaped lynching by an angry crowd; he was arrested by the police, but to universal astonishment acquitted at his trial. The judges could not find that he had actually committed any crime: cremation, it turned out, was legal under British law.

Legal, but definitely not decent, as far as the vast majority of the population were concerned. Price was cremated on his own death 10 years later, but there were to be no further cremations for quite some time. Not until 1902 did London's first designated crematorium open at Golders Green, and even then its

163

Right: Sigmund Freud is among those whose remains are to be found at London's Golders Green crematorium. Once an eccentric choice, cremation is now the norm.

appeal was for a long time very clearly limited to a self-consciously free-thinking and forward-looking intelligentsia. Gothic writer Bram Stoker was burned here in 1912, artist Charles Rennie Mackintosh in 1928, while pioneer psychoanalyst Sigmund Freud and 'sexologist' Havelock Ellis both followed in 1939. These were not the sort of characters from whom Britain's respectable middle classes were likely to take a lead.

Times were changing, though, and with them tastes. The twentieth century brought with it an increasing horror of decay. This was hardly surprising, a mania for hygiene having taken hold. Along with the genuine insights offered by germ theory in the late-nineteenth century, there had been a boom in the manufacture and marketing of labour-saving devices and chemical cleaners, driving up standards of cleanliness in the home. Rugs once taken outside and beaten annually at 'spring-cleaning' were now cleaned with carpet sweepers or vacuum cleaners every day. Families who had once shared earth privies with half the neighbourhood were now acquiring flush-toilets of their own. Though by no means universal, hot and cold running water allowed increasing numbers to bathe far more frequently than ever before; washing machines allowed them to change their clothes. Hygiene was also not just an ethic: it was becoming an aesthetic. The new 'white goods' – refrigerators, washing machines, etc – were indeed dazzling white, and had streamlined shapes for easy cleaning.

Six hundred years before, men and women had dreaded the prospect of dying with the stain of sin upon their souls. Now they feared that they themselves might be the stain. Death, they believed, was dirty. Informed as to the horror of mess and microorganisms, they felt increasingly uneasy about their prospects in the grave. The thought of slow disintegration and the break-out of gaseous bubbling as the body began its decay seemed that much more alarming. Cremation, which involves incinerating the the body at temperatures between 760° and 1150° Celsius (1400–2102° Fahrenheit), so that soft tissue is vaporized and bone reduced to ashes, became the 'modern', clean and convenient solution.

Below: Once shunned by Christians, cremation has been accepted even by the Catholic Church: it now has a definite place in the funereal mainstream.

165

chapter 7

A WORLD OF RITUALS

There is diversity in death. It comes for us all in different ways, depending on our cultural and religious background. No brief survey can even begin to do justice to the extraordinary variety of rituals that have come to surround this concluding, culminating moment of human life. Even within the world's great religions, there are sectarian divisions and local customs that make any attempt at generalization hazardous. Far from being comprehensive, the account that follows can give no more than the merest suggestion of the amazing range of funerary rituals to be found.

ANTIQUE ANTYESHTI

In India's Hindu tradition, there has been clear continuity over many centuries in the conduct of the *Antyeshti,* or cremation. The directions for this, the last of the nine *samskaras,* or sacraments, are laid down in the *Aswalayana Ghryasutra.* This was written down some time around 500 BC, and was probably recording what were already well-established practices. First, the body had to be washed by a member of its own sex. If the body was

Left: Hindu mourners prepare the deceased for death in accordance with the rituals of *Antyeshti,* established in India over many centuries.

167

Right: Funereal customs bind us to our dead, our past – hence their inherent conservatism. In its essentials, the *Antyeshti* has changed little in 3000 years.

that of an adult male, it should first be shaved; then a paste of sandalwood was applied before the deceased was dressed in new clothes. The body was then taken to the pyre, often constructed in a recognized cremation ground, which was generally laid out on the banks of a river. Such a site might well have its own *kunda,* a rectangular fireplace lined with slabs of stone, but this was cleaned and, ideally, purified with cow dung, before use. Alternatively, a trench was dug to contain the fire. The pyre was made of wood and, if these could be afforded, prepared with offerings of sandalwood, saffron, camphor and musk. These would be mixed with ghee – clarified butter – to help them burn.

Lighting the fire was a ritual in itself. First a lamp of ghee was lit, and from this a bit of camphor, which was in turn applied to the pyre at its northernmost end. Once the wood had taken here, it was permissible to work round the rest of the pile until the whole pyre was well alight. At this point, the body was placed on the pyre, its head pointing northward; then it was covered over with wood, and further oblations applied. Large spoons were lashed to long sticks for this purpose. Offerings were made to Agni, the ancient fire-god; to Soma, the deity of plants; to Loka, this World; to the Earth and to the Other World. A further 17 oblations were offered according to the precepts of the Rig Veda and the 63 ordained by the Yajur Veda. These took in everything from the air and the sun to the different parts of the body, emotions such as sadness, and qualities such as hard work and perseverance. The Vedic texts are known to have been written down some time before 1000 BC, so these are venerable ceremonies indeed. From a more prosaic point of view, there were very sound practical reasons for spooning on so much ghee, since this made the fire burn far hotter than it might have done. Burning wood alone does not normally generate enough heat to consume a body completely.

Three days later, when the fire had died and the embers cooled, the family came back for any remaining bones. These were thrown into the river. On the twelfth day after the death, a feast was often held to commemorate the deceased, who from that time on was also to be recalled in the monthly *sraddha* – the celebration of the ancestors. Today, of course, the technology of cremation has been transformed and Hindus have not been slow to embrace these changes, especially those in the big cities. Obviously, under these conditions, oblations cannot be offered, so mantras are repeated in their place.

Sikhs too cremate their dead, the body first being prepared by being washed and then dressed. In death, as in life, the 'Five Ks' must be worn by Sikhs of both sexes. These, as ordained by Guru Gobind Singh in 1699, include *kes* (uncut hair), *kanga* (comb), *kara* (an iron wristband), *kachha* (a special undergarment) and *kirpan* (a special ceremonial dagger). The body is taken to the temple or gurdwara where prayers are said over it, including the *Sukhmani*, or Hymn of Peace. While the body is actually being burned, the traditional bedtime prayer, the Kirtan Soliha, is recited.

Sikhs downplay death, as a mere transition to another life. It is for this reason that extravagant displays of emotion are frowned upon. Instead, the family should withdraw to its home and spend 10 days quietly reading the scripture together. The ashes of the deceased are afterwards collected from the *gurdwara* and, as in Hindu tradition, poured into a nearby river.

EASTERN RITES

Also Indian in its origins, Buddhism was later largely eliminated in the subcontinent, squeezed between the rival religious forces of Hinduism and Islam. While enduring across an extensive swathe of Central, East and Southeast Asia (and in recent times acquiring new adherents in a great many Western countries), Buddhism has to some extent taken on aspects of older indigenous traditions. In China, for example, Buddhism was spiritually influenced by native Daoism – a

Left: Buddhism betrays its Indian origins in the widespread use of cremation, though burial was to become the norm in certain countries.

Right: Reincarnation in action, the Tibetan tradition of 'sky-burial' allows the mortal remains of the dead to be reabsorbed into the natural scheme.

highly philosophical faith whose emphasis on escaping worldly concerns through meditation must have made it seem analogous to the Indian creed in many ways. At the same time, Chinese Buddhism was inevitably influenced by the Confucian code of social teaching, giving it a stronger civic sense than certain other forms of Buddhism.

In many Asian societies, however, Buddhism was imposed from the top down, by rulers who (cynics might suggest) appreciated its doctrine of pacifism as a means of maintaining social order. So, from Tibet to Japan and from Thailand to Korea, we see rather more uniformity than might be expected given the enormous cultural and historical differences between those countries. Within the institutions of Buddhism, there was of course a vigorous debate, leading to the emergence of rival schools, such as Tantric, Theravada, Mahayana and Zen Buddhism. But these did not necessarily part company so emphatically in their attitudes to earthly funeral rituals.

There certainly were differences of detail, however: the practice of 'sky burial' continued in Tibet (*see* Introduction), for example, and the timetable for cremation and subsequent mourning varied greatly. In Japan, now in many ways a highly Westernized society, black suits are worn instead of white for mourning. On the other hand, several ancient customs still hold sway. One of these is the awarding of special new names, or *kaimyo*, to the dead, to prevent their being inadvertently called back as jokes should their mortal name be mentioned. And there are still shrines to be seen in Japanese graveyards at which bereaved parents make offerings, hoping for a better reincarnation for their dead children.

Generally speaking, however, variations on the same basic ceremony are to be seen across the Buddhist world. First, the body is bathed and laid out with incense sticks around it. It is generally placed in a coffin, unlike the Hindu and

Sikh traditions. For the funeral itself, the monks, or *bhikhu,* are summoned to take charge: they play a central role in this as in other rites. On their arrival, offerings are made to them, as a mark of respect to their office, but also in hopes of earning *punya,* or merit, on behalf of the deceased. Often they are seated under a canopy of white cloth – white being the colour of death throughout much of the East. The monks chant blessings over the deceased, and typically prayers are said and a sermon given on the transience of human existence and the promise of rebirth. At this point, the coffin will be closed and transported to the place of cremation (though burial has become traditional in some countries). Once the cremation is complete, a feast is often held – sometimes with raucous, jolly music, to help mourners banish the sadness of bereavement and accept death for the inevitability it is. Further ceremonies are held at appointed intervals (anything between seven days and a month) thereafter until the official mourning cycle is complete.

The various religious strands that have played their part in the formation of funerary tradition in China are very difficult indeed to tease apart. Confucianism, Daoism, Buddhism (and of course, most recently, communism) have all had their impact on attitudes and customs. From the outsider's point of view, however, the most striking thing about Chinese practices is the persistence of a wide range of rituals associated with the ancestors. As we have seen (Chapter 5), offerings are frequently burned with the dead when they are buried. These offerings are regularly renewed at special shrines in the home, where photos are displayed, and incense and further gifts are burned in their honour. Their memorializing at the heart of the family is felt to symbolize their endurance in reincarnation or eternity, as well as bonding those who have been left behind.

Important as such posthumous observances are, the burial process is too important to be left till after death. Many Chinese find it reassuring to know

Left: Japan's cemeteries are every bit as crowded as its cities: these decorated headstones have a distinctly cheerful air.

that their coffin has been bought far in advance of death. If at all possible, the site and position of the tomb are carefully planned according to the principles of *feng shui*. Tombs are often guarded from attack by demons, with statues of Lokapala or spirit warriors being placed outside the entrance. In some traditions, the dead are exhumed after a time, and the bones transferred to a pot. Sometimes this pot is in turn reburied after a period in the open air. The rituals of *ch'ing ming* are very popular: in what amounts to a regular spring cleaning, the tomb is both physically overhauled and spiritually restored with rituals and prayers.

JUDAEO-CHRISTIAN TRADITIONS

The 'Judaeo-Christian tradition' is often regarded as a single continuous sweep, but of course major differences exist between (and within) the two religious systems. While Christians would, for the most part, maintain the Jewish tradition of burying their dead until recently, they went their own way in the accompanying rituals. Chronology was one key area of change. Judaism holds that burial should take place speedily: on the day of death or, failing that, on the day following. This is generally seen as a response to the hot conditions of the Middle East, where Judaism originated – Islam treats its obsequies with similar urgency. There has to be a little more to it than this, though. Hindus and Buddhists in the hotter, more humid regions of India and Southeast Asia are much more leisurely in their approach. The difference would appear to be that the Indian religions believe in reincarnation. They are disposed to see decay not as a slur on the imagined 'integrity' of the deceased, but as an early sign of his or her transition to another state.

From the moment when death descends upon the Jewish household, no time is lost. First a *shemirah,* or vigil, is mounted over the body. The *shomer* – ideally not related to the deceased – keeps up a constant recitation of psalms until it is

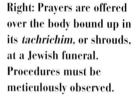

Right: Prayers are offered over the body bound up in its *tachrichim*, or shrouds, at a Jewish funeral. Procedures must be meticulously observed.

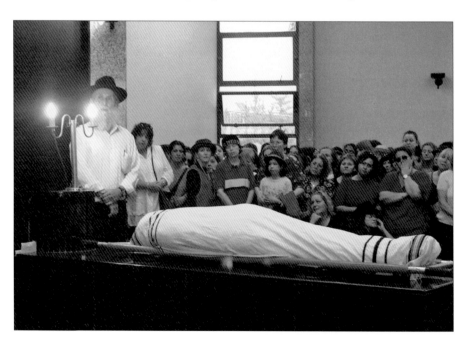

time for the deceased to be interred. Members of the *chevra kadisha,* or local burial society, are called to come and help prepare the body. Their work is strictly voluntary, but pious Jews are proud to be able to perform these duties: care for the dead is seen as especially meritorious since, by definition, it cannot be done with any ulterior motive. They take charge of the *taharah,* ritually cleansing the body with water before wrapping it in white linen *tachrichim,* or shrouds. A man is then traditionally wrapped in his own *tallit,* or prayer-shawl, before the body is placed in the coffin. Fragments of pottery are placed on the eyes and mouth, to symbolize the destruction of the Temple of Jerusalem; earth from Israel is placed inside the casket and on the body to proclaim the occupant's ties with Zion. The coffin is then sealed before the funeral takes place.

This is a simple ceremony, consisting largely of eulogies over the body; further eulogies may be offered at the graveside in the cemetery. Mourners often take turns to shovel earth into the grave. Either just before the funeral or just after it, the ritual of *keriah* is performed: this involves the tearing of a garment. Traditionally, of course, the 'rending of garments' implied the excesses of violent grief, but now a neat tear is made in the clothing. (Sometimes, indeed, it is done still more symbolically, by tearing a ribbon.) On returning home from the cemetery, it is customary for the bereaved family to eat a meal of hardboiled eggs – symbolic, perhaps, of new life to come.

The funeral may be over, but the mourning is just beginning. First comes *shiva* – literally 'seven', the seven-day mourning period prescribed by Jewish law. The term 'sitting Shiva' originates in the fact that mourners are supposed to stay in one place for the duration, although they should leave home to go to synagogue on the Sabbath. They should not have a bath or shower or wear leather shoes or jewellery during *shiva;* men should not shave and mirrors are often kept covered. Often mourners sit on the floor or on low stools to symbolize how debased their bereavement has left them. They receive visits from friends and relations, who bring their memories of the deceased to share.

At the end of seven days, the family surfaces, taking a short walk to mark their re-entry into the world. They are still in mourning, however: throughout the 30-day period of *shiloshim,* men are still not supposed to shave and no mourner is allowed to marry. Restrictions are gradually relaxed through the remainder of the *shanah,* the first year, after which the period of mourning is considered to be at an end.

At the end of the funeral, and regularly thereafter through most of the *shanah,* the *kaddish* is traditionally recited. Though associated with the dead, the *kaddish* makes no mention of loss or sadness but is actually an Aramaic prayer praising God in all His glory, derived from the Bible (Ezekiel, XXXVIII, 23). Ten people (for Orthodox Jews, 10 men) have to be present for it to be offered. They face in the direction of Jerusalem as they speak. It is said monthly for 10 months (in Jewish tradition even the worst soul faces only a year's damnation), but it may also be said on subsequent anniversaries. The end of the *shanah* is also traditionally the time at which the *matzevah* ceremony takes place: the formal unveiling of the headstone on the grave. No flowers are brought to Jewish graveyards since – dying and withering as they do – they are associated not with life and freshness but with transience. Instead small stones are placed on the grave as markers of permanence and durability.

In some traditions, the dead are exhumed after a time, and the bones transferred to a pot. Sometimes this pot is, in turn reburied after a period in the open air.

ETERNAL REST

In Catholic tradition, the mass for the dead is generally known as the Requiem, from the Latin prayer *Requiem aeternam dona eis domine, et lux perpetuam lucean eis...* – Eternal rest, grant unto them O Lord, and let perpetual light shine upon them...

Even in the vernacular, this liturgy is considered to have a special sombre poetry, and the Latin Requiem was to attract inspirational musical settings by composers from Mozart to Verdi and Fauré. For centuries, it contained the famous sequence *Dies Irae,* Day of Anger:

> *Dies irae, dies illa*
> *Solvet saeclum in favilla:*
> *Teste David cum Sibylla.*

Taken from a thirteenth-century poem, this was translated in the Roman Missal of 1962:

> Day of wrath and terror looming!
> Heaven and earth to ash consuming,
> David's word and Sibyl's truth foredooming.

Like Dante's *Inferno,* the *Dies Irae* caught the imagination of Romantic artists. The tune associated with it crops up in works by composers from Brahms and Berlioz to Respighi and Rachmaninov. With the Church itself, however, it was eventually to fall out of favour, being regarded as too grim and frightening to be inflicted on grieving relatives. Except in special circumstances, it has not formed part of the Requiem since the reforms of the Second Vatican Council in 1963. Orthodox Churches had their own equivalents of the Catholic service. The best known, perhaps, is the Russian *Panikhida.*

The various Protestant churches have generally favoured far simpler services. If the uncommitted have often felt the Catholic dead did better on aesthetic grounds, with regard to the Requiem, most have given the Anglican *Book of Common Prayer* the edge with the far shorter committal service that takes place beside the grave:

> Forasmuch as it hath pleased Almighty God of his great mercy to take unto himself the soul of our dear brother/sister here departed, we therefore commit his/her body to the ground; earth to earth, ashes to ashes, dust to dust; in sure and certain hope of the Resurrection to eternal life, through our Lord Jesus Christ; who shall change our vile body, that it may be like unto his glorious body, according to the mighty working, whereby he is able to subdue all things to himself.

The belief in the resurrection of the body meant that cremation was out of the question for Christians until comparatively recently, but attitudes changed in the course of the twentieth century (*see* Chapter 6). Even the Catholic Church, long against the practice, dropped its objections in 1963 at the time of the Second Vatican Council, and it is common among Catholics today.

> **The widow traditionally mourns for a period of four lunar months and 10 days. Some conservatives still say that she should not leave her home – or even her own room – throughout that time.**

174

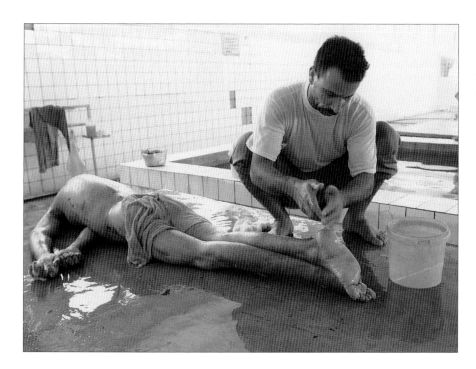

Left: The ritual cleansing of the dead plays an important part in the funerary rites of several of the world's religions.

MUSLIM MOURNING

Salah or *salat* is the generic word for cleanliness or spiritual hygiene under Islam, and it has specific applications in different areas of life. *Janaza Salah* is the name given to the Muslim funeral service, after the *janaza,* or stretcher, on which the body is placed, as soon as possible after death. No coffin is used, and burial is to be organized as quickly as possible. This tradition presumably arose in part because of the practical problems of dealing with a decaying body, but partly too because it was deemed disrespectful to the dead to allow them to decay.

The body is covered over for decency before the *ghusl* or ritual washing takes place. This is done by members of the same sex as the deceased. A set sequence is followed in this ritual cleansing, which begins with the private parts and ends with the feet – first the right and then finally the left. (Martyrs skip the washing stage, because it is important that they should go into the earth with the marks of their martyrdom upon them. For the same reason, they wear the clothes that they were wearing at the time of death.) Once this process is complete, the body can be wrapped in shrouds – different numbers have been used at different times and in different regions and Islamic traditions. Prayers of praise are said to Allah, before the *jazana* is taken to the cemetery for burial, generally on foot. The grave, dug earlier, is orientated so as to allow the deceased to face Mecca. After the body is laid to rest, the grave is filled in and the mourners depart without fuss, since excessive lamentation is traditionally thought to disturb the dead.

The widow mourns for a period of four lunar months and 10 days. Some conservatives still say that she should not leave her home – or even her own room – throughout this time. The original reason for this quarantine was to establish whether she was carrying her late husband's child. Husbands were to leave at least one year's residence and maintenance for wives after their death.

chapter 8

DEATH, PRESENT AND FUTURE

On a blustery day in 1895, an intrepid band of revolutionaries put out from Eastbourne on the south coast of England in a small boat. Eleanor Marx (Karl's widow) and her comrades, however, were not setting sail to liberate the Continent from capitalism, but to consign the mortal remains of Friedrich Engels to the deep. The co-founder of communism had been cremated at Brookwood Cemetery, but had requested this particular end, rejecting the idea of a burial ashore. A generation later, in 1947, two young men set out from further along the same coast, Poole Harbour, Dorset, in a rowing boat that they had hired for the occasion. Once they felt they were far enough out to sea, they together took an urn containing ashes and scattered them upon the lapping waves. The men were half-brothers, Gip Wells and Anthony West, and their common father had been the distinguished writer H.G. Wells. He had in his lifetime been an avowed (and often combative) rationalist and, in his pioneering works of science fiction, a prophet of the future, so it made sense that he should have had no conventional grave. And it was just over a decade after this, in 1958, not far away at Portland Bill, a

Left: The Kennedy and Bessette families watch as the ashes of their relatives, killed in a plane crash, are scattered into the sea off Martha's Vineyard.

Right: Mahmoud
Ahmadinejad, President
of Iran and rival to 'You',
the individual internet-
user, as *Time* magazine's
'person of the year'
for 2006.

spectacular headland, that a woman's ashes were poured into the sea. Though mainly living in London, she had kept a weekend retreat at nearby Easton, and had loved to walk along this wild clifftop. Marie Stopes, a scientist of note after having published some important work on the palaeontology of plants, had shocked the early century with her book on *Married Love* (1918).

Three public figures, then, choosing to be cremated rather than buried, and choosing, furthermore, not to have any specifically locatable final 'resting-place'. At the time, this seemed an eccentric choice, but then these people were hardly conventional characters – all three, indeed, were arguably more notorious than famous in the normal sense. What a communist leader, a radical freethinker and an unabashed birth-control campaigner chose to do with their ashes was their own concern, of course: no respectable people would have taken their cue from them. For better or for worse, though, all these individuals were in some sense to see their visions realized – Engels, perhaps, for the worse. Yet, just as space-travel and contraception were to pass imperceptibly from the realm of the unthinkable to the utterly familiar, so too would this futuristic way with mortal remains.

POSTMODERN MORTALITY

Never before have we as individuals seemed so powerful as in recent years, controlling and customizing almost every aspect of our lives.

'You', *Time* magazine proclaimed at the end of 2006, are the 'Person of the Year', joining a prestigious list that started in 1927 with aviator Charles Lindbergh. Previous titleholders had included Franklin D. Roosevelt, John F. Kennedy, Mikhail Gorbachev and Pope John Paul II (and, for that matter, Josef Stalin and Adolf Hitler). This time, a reflective cover allowed the reader to see his or her own face looking back, as though in a mirror, from that hotly contested spot on the front of the famous journal. True, *Time* subsequently conceded, 'you' had only narrowly pipped Iran's President Mahmoud Ahmadinejad to the position, but most commentators agreed with the decision. It was only right and proper for the ordinary person, empowered by the internet, to push America's current foreign-policy bogeyman into second place.

Never before have we as individuals seemed so powerful as in recent years, controlling and customizing almost every aspect of our lives. Many of our choices may be illusory, of course, restricted to retail purchases and 'lifestyle' choices, but our sense of autonomy is very strong. Through the power of the computer and the worldwide web, we can be 'consulted' every day by business and government – however, little notice is actually taken of our views. By using 'interactive' broadcasting and online media, we can participate in ongoing debates and discussions on everything from politics to sport. Such media have even set us free us from what we always thought of as inescapable realities, allowing us to assume fresh identities of whatever sort we choose. We can take part in Internet sex-chat, under whatever names we choose and claiming to be however much younger, thinner and fitter than we really are. We can, if we so desire, change our sex and nationality, and no one who knows our online 'self' need be any the wiser. These personas are no more than virtual, of course, but even so they would have astonished our forebears, whose fantasy-selves were never given even a fraction of the validation ours enjoy. Like many liberations, it brings with it disorientation; empowering as it is, it is often scary. The more we can intervene to fashion a media in our own image, the more internet 'I's' we can

Above: Gardens of Remembrance have been replacing graveyards as resting-places of the dead and repositories of memories.

command, the less secure our actual sense of who we are.

It may have taken technology to bring about this change, but the world was well ready for it when it came. Literary theorists and philosophers have for decades been talking about the primacy of language over the 'objective' reality it supposedly describes. Words, they say, do not refer to a pre-existing reality; rather, the way our culture describes our world defines the way it 'is'. Our own 'selves', by the same token, are the constructions of our culture; there is no 'inner' self, or soul, as such. We may feel we somehow transcend the society and culture that have produced us, but actually they drive our lives, our consciousness, who we are, what we think and feel. We may not as individuals accept that we have truly been 'decentred' in this way, but there is no doubt that as a society we have tended to behave as though we have. Long before this sensibility was evident in our media, it was becoming clear from the decisions people were making about what they wanted to happen to their mortal remains.

LOCATION, LOCATION, LOCATION

The grave has been going out of fashion. In Britain, for example, cremation was almost unheard of in 1900; in 1946, 50,000 people took this option. An impressive rise, perhaps, but from a negligible base: the vast majority of men and women still chose burial. Since that time, however, the situation has been transformed: today, 72 per cent of people are burned to ashes.

What happens to those ashes has changed as well: for a long time, most were reverently placed in the Garden of Remembrance attached to the crematorium. There, they might as well have been buried, decomposition apart: there were markers to say who they were and when they had lived and, of course, they were 'placed' for as long as it could matter at a particular spot. There are far worse places to end up – such gardens are often beautifully laid out and painstakingly maintained – and most people were well satisfied with this choice. In the 1970s, as Emma Cook reported recently in the *Guardian* newspaper (19 August 2006), 88 per cent of those cremated were disposed of in this way. Only 12 per cent had their ashes taken away by family members.

Today, almost 60 per cent of ashes are taken away to be given a more personalized ending than the flower beds and shrubberies of the Garden of Remembrance garden afford. People no longer wish to be placed, 'pinned down' by a tombstone, or even by a little namecard in a Garden of Remembrance, however serene the surroundings. Rather, they want their final destiny on earth to evoke the specifics of their lifetimes: views they have loved, their family holidays, their fishing trips and football matches. These are the aspects of their lives that they feel make them 'what they are', and it has become important now, as never before, that these aspects should be recalled in death. The place where you walked the dog; where you and your partner first kissed, where your dead child loved to play: these are the sites of mourning for a generation whose members have wanted to take more control over how they will be regarded by those who survive them. If our end helps to define our life as a whole, then the setting in which we wind up can play a key part in that, offering a 'frame' through which we will be seen in memory.

In December 2006, for example, Walter Palfrey died in Pershore, near Worcester, England. Before his retirement, he had taught at the local High School for 36 years. As a beloved member of the school community for so long, it seemed appropriate to his family that his ashes should be scattered in its grounds. Just over a decade before, in 1995, the ashes of railway engineer Roy Hughes were placed in a tunnel deep beneath the streets of Liverpool. He had spent years campaigning for, and then had finally designed, a rail-loop connecting up the city's various different suburban lines, so it made sense somehow for his remains to end up here. Walker and writer Alfred Wainwright did much to promote the beauties of northern England's Lake District. On his death in 1991, his ashes were scattered above the village of Buttermere, on the slopes of his favourite mountain, Haystacks.

Below: In life, Nelva Mendez de Falcone fought for 'people power', demonstrating in Buenos Aires's Plaza de Mayo; in death she expressed that power, having her ashes sprinkled there.

Above: The ashes of fashion photographer Helmut Newton are accompanied by his widow June to a resting-place beside the grave of sometime subject Marlene Dietrich.

Across the Atlantic in Buenos Aires, Nelva Mendez de Falcone died in 2006. She had become famous as one of the 'Mothers of the Plaza de Mayo'. They had met weekly in the Argentinean capital's main square, holding silent protests to demand information on what had happened about their missing sons and daughters, the *Desaparecidos* who had disappeared in the course of the 'Dirty War' waged by the military dictatorship of the 1970s and early '80s. Though the *Desaparecidos* were presumed dead, their remains were for the most part never to be discovered – many were believed to have been dumped from special 'Death Flights' over the sea. But, while her body might physically disappear, Nelva was never to be allowed to vanish in the same way: some of her ashes were sprinkled in the Plaza de Mayo.

Sport is no longer a pastime but a religion, it is often said, and famous stadiums have become shrines of sorts. Many men in particular aspire to have their ashes sprinkled on the 'hallowed turf' or buried around the perimeters of the pitches on which they saw their greatest dramas acted out. While such arrangements were unusual at first (and venues were happy enough to oblige, and avail themselves of the press publicity), the custom caught on, and has become increasingly problematic. Several of Britain's most famous football grounds have been forced to reject applications on behalf of their teams' dead fans, overwhelmed by the sheer number of such requests.

In 2006, the American musician Meatloaf announced that he was going to have his ashes scattered across the pitch of New York's Yankee Stadium when he died. But he had to reach his own special arrangement with the management of the Bronx venue for this, and it was clear that he was to be the exception, rather than the rule.

CREMATORY COMPLICATIONS

As the examples above show, our new-found freedoms cannot be unlimited. There are already signs, indeed, that they bring their costs. No major sports stadium can seriously double as an unofficial cemetery in the longer term, but who, in that case, should be admitted and who refused? Are we going to find ourselves in a situation in which, as with the local church in former times, only dignitaries get to occupy the favoured places inside? And what happens when there is a change in circumstances? Liverpool Football Club, whose supporters are considered to be among the most devoted in the world, were in 2007 about

Below: Wales's highest mountain, Snowdon has withstood the worst rigours of the weather through countless centuries – but it could be rendered barren by the sprinkling of ashes, ecologists fear.

183

to leave their famous Anfield ground for a purpose-built stadium nearby. Along with all the other challenges of relocation, they faced the challenge of what to do about the ashes of so many supporters who had been allowed to be buried beneath the 'hallowed turf'.

At what was the Ocean Cove caravan site, near Tintagel on the coast of Cornwall, a new developer has been making changes, replacing the family caravans in favour of permanent lodges likely to cater for young professionals without children. A controversial move to begin with, of course, but still more so than it might have been, as Steven Morris writes in the *Guardian* (23 October 2006). One longstanding visitor, Janet Oakley-Hills, we are told 'scattered her mother's ashes at Ocean Cove, and wants her children to do the same with her remains. But she will never again be able to stay at the spot.'

Yet commercial considerations are not the only ones likely to pose problems in the future. Environmental concerns have already been raised. In 2006, Emma Cook notes:

> the Mountaineering Council of Scotland asked bereaved relatives to avoid the most popular sites on Scottish summits because of worries that the volume of ashes was causing soil changes. In Leicestershire, boaters on the River Soar complained that if mourners continue to sprinkle ashes there, it will become unusable. Similarly conservation officers on Snowdon [Wales's highest mountain] recently asked people to consider alternatives because of the ecological effects on the vegetation.

As 'green' consciousness grows, so too does alarm at the toxic emissions –

Right: New century, new funerary rite: 'green' burials offer a real alternative to a generation schooled in the values of ecology.

BROCKLANDS
Woodland
Burial

including mercury – which crematoria release into the atmosphere. For the ecologically aware, it seems, burial is back. Decomposition holds no terrors for a generation schooled in James Lovelock's Gaia Hypothesis and thus accustomed to see the earth as a single organism, stable in its cycles of constant change. Nor are 'Neo-Pagans' likely to worry about their bodies breaking down to be reabsorbed into Nature's never-ending flux. Not, of course, that old-fashioned cemeteries will do. Their regimentation apart, these are ecological disaster spots: their mechanically mowed and pesticide-saturated lawns are just the start. Conventional undertakers leave a significant 'carbon footprint' with their steel-framed coffins, which are finished with hardwoods often derived from threatened forests in the tropics. The chemicals with which bodies are embalmed are unlikely to do the earth any good at all, especially when formaldehyde seeps out into the water table.

Above: The British nation said it with flowers after the death of Diana, Princess of Wales in 1997, which sparked a remarkable outpouring of grief.

In today's 'eco-cemetery', then, a body is buried in a biodegradable textile shroud or cardboard coffin; the grave is typically marked by a tree rather than a headstone. Ideally, the grass is not cut but rather is left, to be colonized by wild flowers and animals, an overall 'eco-system' of which the deceased becomes a part.

NEW WAYS OF GRIEVING

If attitudes to burial have been transformed, what about our views of death and mourning? Many commentators believe that these have been changing too. In the United Kingdom, it was widely felt that some sort of watershed had been reached with the reaction to the death of Diana, Princess of Wales in 1997. Millions mourned the media-friendly princess after she was killed in a car accident in Paris, her death comprehensively up-staging that of Mother Teresa of Calcutta just the day before. Floral offerings stretched as far as the eye could see outside her Kensington Palace home. Women – and men – wept openly: it was all very un-English, it was generally agreed, though such assertions are surely unreliable, given the state funerals for Horatio Nelson and the Duke of Wellington. Crowds queued to sign the 'condolence book' there, but further books were opened at town halls and shopping centres across the land. On the day of the funeral itself, three million mourners flocked into London, to witness one of the most extraordinary spectacles the capital had ever seen.

Pop star Elton John sang at the funeral service, which was held in Westminster Abbey, while a vast crowd watched proceedings on screens outside. Earl Spencer drew indecorous cheers from those listening in the street with some scarcely veiled criticisms of the Royal Family's treatment of his sister. This was o be a developing theme: the 'outpouring of grief' took on an ugly quality, it was widely felt, in the days that followed as resentment grew that the Queen was not showing sufficient feeling at Diana's death. Several commentators voiced the sense that there was something coercive about all this sentiment, that their reactions were being monitored by the 'Grief Police'. And over the ensuing months and years, many came to feel that what they saw as a 'hysteria', whipped up by the media, had licensed a more general slide into sentimentality. Every public figure who died had to be extravagantly mourned, they complained, whilst floral shrines sprang up by roadsides for accident victims – an unprecedented thing.

It is difficult, however, to say whether anything had really changed in the British national character, still less in human nature as a whole. What is clear, perhaps, is that in what was already becoming an 'interactive' age, men and women expected their losses to be registered by society at large, just as they expected to be allowed to have their own stake in the tragedies of public figures. Increasingly, indeed, the media have made facilities available so that their consumers can record their thoughts on any personage's passing, everything from radio phone-ins to tribute links on news websites. 'No man is an island,' wrote the sixteenth-century poet John Donne, and that has never seemed truer than it does today, even if, as some suspect, this is due more to voyeurism than true sympathy.

That medicine might one day do away with death remains as fanciful as ever, most would feel, but there are some exciting innovations.

A LIFE AFTER DEATH?

It seems a safe assumption that the freethinkers with whom we began this chapter would have been surprised to learn that religion would be alive and well at the start of the twenty-first century. Indeed, religion is arguably growing stronger in many places, including both the Islamic world and North America. There has certainly been no sign of the wholesale collapse in faith that was long predicted. Many, then, do look forward 'in sure and certain hope of the Resurrection to eternal life', in the words of the Anglican Church's *Book of Common Prayer*. They may be less likely than previous generations to envisage an afterlife in a quasi-geographical place, but they are as confident as ever that death is not the end.

Other people remain more sceptical, just as many have been throughout modernity – the Enlightenment has certainly left its mark. Yet even for such people, the absolute finality of death has in certain respects been called into question as the demarcation between life and death has become more blurred. Recent advances in medical science have offered cures for once-untreatable illnesses and allow an unprecedented degree of control over the trajectory of terminal decline. If death has not been 'conquered' in the sense of being abolished altogether, doctors have to some extent usurped its role in dictating the moment at which life will end.

Increasingly patients have taken a measure of control over their own destinies. Once viewed as an abomination, euthanasia is now seen by many in the developed world as not just permissible but the civilized option for adults facing the pain and indignity of a terminal illness. Many disagree, of course – and there have been prosecutions over cases of 'doctor-assisted suicide'. But for some the ability to produce a 'Living Will', authorizing euthanasia under certain

That medicine might one day do away with death remains as fanciful as ever, most would feel, but there are some exciting innovations. Recent work on DNA and the Human Genome Project has shed light on many of life's mysteries, but the research has yet to tell us how we might forestall its extinction. At the same time, research into stem cells, which can be encouraged to reproduce themselves in many different forms, repairing damaged tissue of every kind, has opened up all sorts of possibilities. As yet, however, there is no sign that these include immortality.

Some adherents of cryonic 'science' refuse to be discouraged. They still harbour the hope that in the instant of death their bodies might be flash-frozen, then kept secure for however long it takes for the skills and technology to become available that will restore and reanimate them. Others look to cloning – though the replication of one's body, however perfect, is hardly the same as the resurrection of one's own self. Most of us would feel that we are the sum of our own insights and experiences: our copy would be another person, as far as we were concerned.

At least for the moment, then, it seems we must be content to submit to the inevitability of death, just as our predecessors have through countless generations. We too will have to face what they have faced, no doubt feeling all the fears they felt, and with no better sense than they of what awaits us, if anything. In the end, a history of death can offer no comfort for the bereaved, nor any counsel that will ease the event itself. Yet it is a consolation of a sort to see the myriad ways in which death, with all its terrors, has enriched our human cultures over so many centuries. As a rite of passage, a rounding-off – even just as an impending threat that helps 'concentrate the mind' – death has given definition to our lives.

Below: Founder of Methodism John Wesley watches an eighteenth-century experiment with electricity: science has yet to supplant religion when it comes to explaining mortality.

BIBLIOGRAPHY

Alighieri, Dante, tr. John D. Sinclair. *The Divine Comedy: 1. Inferno.* Oxford: OUP, 1939.
— *The Divine Comedy: 2. Purgatorio.* Oxford: OUP, 1939.
— *The Divine Comedy: 3. Paradiso.* Oxford: OUP, 1946.
Allan, Tony. *Vikings: The Battle at the End of Time.* London: Duncan Baird Publishing, 2002.
Arnold, Catharine. *Necropolis: London and Its Dead.* London: Simon & Schuster, 2006.
Arrian, tr. E.I. Robson. *Anabasis of Alexander.* Cambridge, MA: Loeb Classical Library, 1929.

Barley, Nigel. *Dancing on the Grave: Encounters with Death.* London: John Murray, 1995.
Binski, Paul. *Medieval Death: Ritual and Representation.* London: British Museum Press, 1996.
Bowker, John, ed. *Cambridge Illustrated History of Religions.* Cambridge: Cambridge University Press, 2002.
— *Oxford Dictionary of World Religions.* Oxford: Oxford University Press, 1997.

Camp, John M., and Elizabeth Fisher. *The World of the Ancient Greeks.* London: Thames & Hudson, 2002.

De Vries, Leonard, ed. *History as Hot News: The World of the Early Victorians Through the Eyes of the 'Illustrated London News', 1842–65.* London: John Murray, 1995.
Diodorus Siculus, tr. C.H. Oldfather. *Diodorus of Sicily.* Cambridge, MA: Loeb Classical Library, 1934.
Durkheim, Émile. *The Elementary Forms of Religious Life.* Oxford: OUP, Oxford World's Classics, 2001.

Evans, Susan Toby. *Ancient Mexico and Central America: Archaeology and Culture History.* London: Thames & Hudson, 2004.

Freeman, J. D. *Report on the Iban.* London: Athlone, 1970.

Gillespie, Susan D. 'Body and Soul Among the Maya: Keeping the Spirits in Place'. *Archaeological Papers of the American Anthropological Association,* Vol. 11, no. 1, 2002.
Green, Miranda J. *Exploring the World of the Druids.* London: Thames & Hudson, 1997.

Herodotus, tr. A. de Selincourt. *The Histories.* Rev'd with Introduction and Notes by A.R. Burn. London: Penguin, 1983.
Hodder, Ian. *Çatalhöyük: The Leopard's Tale – Revealing the Mysteries of Turkey's Ancient Town.* London: Thames & Hudson, 2006.
— 'This Old House'. *Natural History,* June 2006.
Huntington, Richard, and Peter Metcalf. *Celebrations of Death: The Anthropology of Mortuary Ritual.* Cambridge: CUP, 1979.

Ibn Battuta, tr. Sir Hamilton Gibb. *The Travels of Ibn Battuta, AD 1325–1354.* Cambridge: Hakluyt Society/CUP, 1971.

Kerrigan, Michael. *Who Lies Where: A Guide to Famous Graves.* London: Fourth Estate, 1995.

Landa, Fray Diego de. Relación de las Cosas de Yucatán (www.wayeb.org/download/resources/landa.pdf)
Lewis-Williams, J. David and David Pierce. *Inside the Neolithic Mind: Consciousness, Cosmos and the Realm of the Gods.* London: Thames & Hudson, 2005.
Lucan, tr. Robert Graves. *Pharsalia.* Harmondsworth: Penguin, 1956.

Magowan, Fiona. 'Syncretism or Synchronicity? Remapping the Yolngu Feel of Place'. *Australian Journal of Anthropology,* December 2001.
Milligan, Max. *Realm of the Incas.* London: HarperCollins, 2001.

Plutarch, tr. Ian Scott-Kilvert. *The Age of Alexander.* Harmondsworth: Penguin, 1973.

Reeves, Nicholas. *The Complete Tutankhamun: The King. The Tomb. The Royal Treasure.* London: Thames & Hudson, 2007.
Richardson, Ruth. *Death, Dissection and the Destitute: The Politics of the Corpse in Pre-Victorian Britain.*

Salomon, Frank. 'Testimonies: The Making and Reading of Native South American Historical Sources'. *The Cambridge History of the Native Peoples of the Americas. Volume III, South America.* Cambridge: Cambridge University Press, 1999.
Scott, Ronnie. *Death by Design: The True Story of the Glasgow Metropolis.* Edinburgh: Black & White Publishing, 2005.
Strabo, tr. H.L. Jones. *The Geography of Strabo.* Cambridge, MA: Loeb Classical Library, 1923.

Taylor, Anne Christine. 'Remembering to Forget: Identity, Mourning and Memory Among the Jivaro'. *Man,* December 1993.
Taylor, Timothy. *The Buried Soul: How Humans Invented Death.* London: Fourth Estate, 2002.
Turner, Alice K. *The History of Hell.* London: Robert Hale, 1993.
Tyldesley, Joyce A. *Chronicle of the Queens of Egypt: From Earliest Times to the Death of Cleopatra.* London: Thames & Hudson, 2006.

Vitebsky, Piers. *Reindeer People: Living with Animals and Spirits in Siberia.* London: HarperCollins, 2005.

Winter, Jay. *Sites of Memory, Sites of Mourning: The Great War in European Cultural History.* Cambridge: Cambridge University Press, 1995.
Woolf, Greg, ed. *Cambridge Illustrated History of the Roman World.* Cambridge: Cambridge University Press, 2003.
—, ed. *Ancient Civilizations: The Illustrated Guide to Belief, Mythology and Art.* London: Duncan Baird Publishing, 2005.

INDEX

PICTURE CREDITS

Art Archive: 79, 88

Corbis: 6/7 (Gideon Mendel), 7 (Bettmann), 10 (Roman Soumar), 11 (Della Zuana Pascal), 13 (Fine Art Photographic Library), 14 (Michael Nicholson), 19 (Bettmann), 20 (Alain Le Garsmeur), 23 (Christel Gerstenberg), 25 (Dean Conger), 26 (Tibor Bognár), 27 (Gianni Dagli Orti), 28 (Richard A. Cooke), 29 (Roger Wood), 31 (Christophe Boisvieux), 32, 33 (Alinari Archives), 34 (Bettmann), 36 (Dave G. Houser), 39 (Sakamoto Photo Research Laboratory), 40 (Werner Forman), 42 (Aladin Abdel Naby), 44 (Roger Wood), 45 (Gianni Dagli Orti), 48 (Charles & Josette Lenars), 51 (Bettmann), 52 (Sandro Vannini), 53 (Sandro Vannini), 54 (Sandro Vannini), 57 (Historical Picture Archive), 59 (Mimmo Jodice), 61 (Bettmann), 62 (Bettmann), 64 (Gianni Dagli Orti), 66 (Sandro Vannini), 69 (Historical Picture Archive), 71 (Historical Picture Archive), 73 (Lindsay Hebberd), 74 (Raheb Homavandi), 80 (Elio Ciol), 81 (Chris Hellier), 82 (David Lees), 84 (Bettmann), 87 (Bettmann), 90 (Hulton-Deutsch Collection), 91 (Archivo Iconografico, S.A.), 93 (Nik Wheeler), 94 (Danny Lehman), 97 (Yann Arthus-Bertrand), 98 (Ilya Naymushin), 99 (Stapleton Collection), 100 (Lindsay Hebberd), 103 (Yann Arthus-Bertrand), 104 (Gallo Images), 106 (Bettmann), 108 (Bettmann), 109 (Ivan Alvarado), 111 (Pablo Corral Vega), 112 (Roger Antrobus), 117 (Amit Bhargava), 121 (Sandro Vannini), 122 (Patrick Bennett), 125 (Caroline Penn), 127 (Werner Forman), 129 (Christophe Boisvieux), 130 (Bettmann), 134 (Free Agents Limited), 137 (Arte & Immagini srl), 138 (Bettmann), 141 (Bettmann), 149 (Wild Country), 150 (Seamas Culligan), 158 (Catherine Karnow), 161 (Dave Bartruff), 170 (Craig Lovell), 171 (Red James), 172 (Reuters), 175 (Jehad Nga), 176 (Reuters), 181 (Carrion Carlos), 182 (Wolfgang Kumm), 183 (Colin McPherson), 184 (Ashley Cooper), 185 (Ralf-Finn Hestoft)

Mary Evans Picture Library: 17, 144, 146, 152, 157, 164 (Sigmund Freud Copyrights), 187

Getty Images: 9 (Robert Harding), 56 (Hulton Archive), 68/69 (Scott Warren), 76 (Time Life Pictures), 116 (Scott Peterson), 118 (Hoang Dinh Nam), 128 (MPI), 133 (Kirby/Hulton Archive), 143 (Leonard McCombe), 154 (Hulton Archive), 160 (Evening Standard), 166 (Dibyangshu Sarkar), 168 (Sebastian D'Souza), 169 (Andrea Pistolesi), 179 (Atta Kenare)

Rex Features: 165 (Richard Gardner), 180 (The Travel Library)

Topfoto: 24 (Delitz/HIP), 113, 114 (Woodmansterne), 131, 151

US Department of Defense/US Navy: 163

Werner Forman Archive Ltd: 47